Selves in Action

How different parts of us inform and influence our daily lives

John Kent

First Printing, February 2012

ISBN 978-1-4716-2166-6

Contents

Foreword

It has been 40 years since we met and began our journey of discovery into Voice Dialogue and the Psychology of Selves. Our explorations were a good deal of hard work and a good deal of fun and the territory we were traveling was very new and uncharted. Today there are many teachers and facilitators who are working with these issues and the number of books and articles has proliferated in a remarkable way, something that is of great satisfaction to us.

We are pleased to introduce this new book by John Kent entitled "Selves in Action". The main body of the book is a compilation of the pieces he has been writing on his blog for a number of years. What he has done in these writings is to go back in his life and show the reader how different selves have shown up for him in the everyday living of his life. He has broken these vignettes into certain basic themes that he then discusses from his perspective as the one who is awakening to - and having to deal with - these various selves.

When it comes to personal growth, there seems to be no substitute for telling one's personal story. And John is a delightful storyteller. His stories embrace both the personal emotional experience of the selves and the ways in which he (and his strong cognitive faculties) was able to deal with these selves as he became conscious of them.

The selves, after all, are no great mystery. They are always present. The primary selves are always running our lives and the disowned selves are always trying to break through and get our attention. Yet it is still a reality that many people do not have any awareness or understanding that these selves even exist. For instance, they go on living with amazingly low self-esteem and, by and large, have no comprehension that there is a voice within - an Inner-Critic - that is constantly saying terrible things to them. If they knew this, they could deal with it in a new and different way. John's stories of the selves help to bring these selves to awareness.

The style of John's book is easy to read and it would be appropriate to any level of psycho-spiritual development. It is eminently readable just *because* it is so personal and so human. It is about the awakening of the Aware Ego process in him and the clarity and the richness that this brings to his life. We can see and feel his selves in action and, as he becomes more and more conscious of them, we can feel the evolution of the Aware Ego process. Lastly, we can share in his experience and see how this process has never stopped for him.

We have known John for many years and we wish him well in this new publishing venture. It is our feeling that "Selves in Action" will awaken the consciousness of Selves in many people and deepen the process already happening for many other travelers on this path.

We send our love to John and to all of the people who are already related to this way of viewing the world. And we happily invite newcomers to experience the great "turning on of the lights" ceremony when they make that first wonderful discovery: "Oh my God – I never knew *that* was a self!"

Drs. Hal and Sidra Stone

Albion, California

February, 2012

www.voicedialogue.org

Acknowledgements

Heartfelt thanks to Hal and Sidra Stone for birthing Voice Dialogue and giving the gift of the Aware Ego Process so freely and generously to the world. I value their love and support. Thanks to Gail Steuart who first introduced me to Voice Dialogue and started me on my journey of selves discovery. I owe many of my facilitation skills to her. A huge debt of gratitude to Michael Zimmerman for his encouragement and the many hours he has devoted to reviewing and suggesting changes and improvements to the manuscript. His Inner Editor is truly awesome. Finally, a big thank you to all my students and clients from whom I have learnt so much.

Kew, London
February 2012

1
Introduction

Our many selves

Do you ever hear yourself say, "A part of me....", as in:

"A part of me wants to tell people exactly what I think, but another part is scared I'll upset them and stops me from saying anything at all."

On radio and TV you will often hear people using expressions like: *"A part of me", "I push myself", "I'm in two minds"*. Ads are constantly encouraging us to develop our inner Warriors, Lovers, Geeks, Adventurers - and more! In each of these words and phrases there is an implicit understanding that we are all made up of many different parts or "selves."

In the late 1970's, ground-breaking therapists, Drs. Hal & Sidra Stone, developed an original and highly transformational approach to personal growth they called Voice Dialogue. This safe and simple process enables us to tune in to our different selves and allow their voices to be heard more clearly and distinctly. So, where do these selves come from?

Primary selves

No matter into which culture we are born we all share a common human experience: *vulnerability*. The human baby is born vulnerable and must be taken care of by others in order to survive. This means each of us has to develop a personality that will get our essential needs met from the adults around us. These needs can be summarised as:

Attention - notice me and take care of me

Approval - show me that you like and accept my way of being and doing

Affection - love me

The three **A**'s never go away. Our Vulnerable self remains with us our entire life and much of our adult behaviour is unconsciously driven by its core needs. Just think how you would feel today if you walked into a room and nobody noticed you; or if people told you that they disapproved of your behaviour, style, or way of being; or if someone close to you said that they didn't care about you or even hated you! Ouch!!

Your vulnerability would be touched, causing you to feel intense emotional pain.

To handle our vulnerability and get these basic needs met we begin to develop a personality made up of a group of protecting selves. These dominant or *primary selves* look around and notice what behaviour is rewarded and what is punished. They figure out the rules of our specific family, environment and culture, and have us behave in ways that are most likely to get the adults around us to satisfy our needs.

Our primary selves - which can shift and change as our life circumstances change - are unique to each of us. However, generic examples might be:

Pleaser: *"You must always be nice to others."*

Pusher: *"You must work hard to succeed."*

Responsible: *"You must act appropriately."*

These primary selves - each with it's own voice - form a powerful *operating system*. They run our lives and determine our values, attitudes, beliefs and behaviours. As we grow up they colour the way we see others and also how others see us. They determine what we like and dislike and what we judge and don't judge. For most of us our operating system *is* us. We are identified with it. It is who we think we are. But that is only half the picture.

Hidden selves

There is no up without down, no fast without slow, no happy without sad. Life is full of these dualities. So for every primary self that we identify with there has to be an opposite self that we have more or less hidden away, buried, or *disowned*. Opposites of the above examples might be:

Selfish: *"You must put your own needs first."*

Easy-Going: *"Relax, kick back, things will take care of themselves."*

Rebellious: *"Don't do what is expected of you."*

The more strongly we identify with a particular primary self, the more deeply we have to bury its opposite energy. Remember: the job of our primary selves is to protect our vulnerability. They are terrified that their opposites will come out and cause problems. Their worst fear is that people around us will see these disowned selves and withdraw their attention, approval and affection from us. People will say for example, *"How could you be so selfish / lazy / disrespectful?!"*

Using attraction and judgement to learn about our selves

Most of us are so identified with the primary selves that run our lives that we have no idea that these opposite selves are alive and well and living somewhere inside us. Imagine a woman who has developed a very strong Pleaser self. She always feels driven to be nice to other people, help them in any way she can and make sure that they are happy. This was what was demanded of her as she grew up in her original family. If ever she was not nice to other people and put herself first she felt the intense negative judgements of the adults around her.

Typically she might meet a man who is the opposite of her. He will be more self-centred and be able to say "no" to the demands of others. He will be able to set clear boundaries and be able to ask people to do things for him without worrying about their feelings all the time. She may be irresistibly and mysteriously attracted to him. Or she may feel very judgemental towards him for being so selfish, self-serving and insensitive to others. She may even marry him and spend her life alternating between attraction (a *positive bonding pattern*[1]) and judgement (a *negative bonding pattern*)!

What is going on in this example? There is an old proverb that says, *"When we point the finger of judgement at another person there are three fingers pointing back to us"*. Judgements come from our primary selves. It is the woman's Pleaser who judges those "selfish" people. Whenever we feel a judgement towards another person we need to pay attention to the particular trait or traits that we are judging because this will tell us what selves we are identified with and what selves we have therefore disowned.

In a Voice Dialogue session[2] we can learn how to separate from our primary selves and find out the rules they have for running our lives. We can learn and understand their demands, hopes and anxieties. This means that we need no longer be overly influenced by their default attitudes, values, beliefs and behaviours. Only then are we able to become more aware of the opposite disowned selves within us and find a space to stand between them where we can exercise conscious choice. This space we call the Aware Ego.

The Aware Ego process

Every time we access and then separate from a primary or disowned self we enter into and strengthen the Aware Ego. For example, if you are strongly identified with your Pusher and then you separate from it, the "you" that began the Voice Dialogue session is no longer the same "you"

[1] See Glossary, Appendix 2

[2] See Facilitation, Appendix 1

because you are no longer identified with your Pusher. You are then free to go to the other side and access your Easy-Going self, understand its motivation and then separate from it. When you come back to centre you are again a new "you" - one that is now no longer identified with your Pusher or with your Easy-Going self. Resting between these two is the Aware Ego.

The Aware Ego is constantly in process - a process of learning to stand in the space between opposites. Since we are all made up of literally hundreds of different selves, the process is a dynamic one and continually evolving. There is always something new to learn about our selves. It is truly a process of compassion for every aspect of our psyche in which none are judged as good or bad. This inevitably increases our capacity for awareness (the traditional witness position of the meditator), acceptance and appropriate action.

Selves in action

In this collection of short biographical essays - originally written as blogs - I will give you examples of my selves in action. As you read about my journey of selves-discovery and how different parts of me have informed and influenced my life, I invite you to consider your own selves. Which parts of you have been in charge of "driving your bus" as you travel through life? How have they served you? Have any selves been excluded as a consequence? Which of your selves have interacted with others in your relationships - both in positive and negative ways? How might your experience of life be different if you could become aware of and embrace more of your selves?

I have grouped the essays thematically and not in chronological order. Each one stands alone as a description of a particular experience in my life, so feel free to dip in and out as you wish. To help you understand the Voice Dialogue lens through which I am viewing these experiences, please take a look at the appendices where you will find a description of a Voice Dialogue session, a glossary of Voice Dialogue terms and suggested reading, viewing, and websites to browse.

Enjoy your selves!

2

THE JOURNEY OF
SELVES DISCOVERY

Life has a habit of bringing us opportunities to wake up to the multiplicity of who we are - the "we" behind the "I". Such opportunities can be found in major life events - changing jobs, moving house, starting a new relationship or a family - as well as in our every day encounters at work, while out shopping, sitting in a café, or travelling on a bus or plane. If we are open to what life brings us, we discover there's a kind of organising intelligence, inviting us to get to know our selves better.

The Crucible

In the mid 80's I was introduced to an Englishman who had a management training business based in Munich. Paul ran programmes for German business people aimed at improving their cross-cultural communication skills. We hit it off immediately and soon began developing and running intensive workshops together.

The German business milieu values order, detail and discipline, and I felt very much at home. I was good at organising and planning, and loved the process of creating new programmes. We worked and reworked the structure, content, timing and delivery of each workshop until they were perfect. We impressed clients with our logical explanations, clear paradigms and comprehensive models. No request was too much for us and we drove ourselves relentlessly. A typical seminar day began at 8am and did not end until the last participant left the hotel bar, often after midnight. Our German participants thought we were *"Wunderbar!"*

In the third year of our cooperation Paul and I trained 180 days in fifty locations. This did not include the days spent in development, preparation and travel. Professionally and financially I had become very successful, but I was beginning to feel an emptiness inside. I had no time for a social life or to develop intimate relationships. Something told me I should take a break or I might I burn out.

I negotiated a three-month sabbatical with Paul, devised a detailed itinerary, bought a round-the-world air ticket and headed off - first stop S.E. Asia. I had lived and worked in the region before, so there were lots of people I wanted to see, as well as a long list of new destinations to visit. After a hectic six weeks of sightseeing in Singapore, Thailand, Hong Kong and Japan, I flew to Hawaii to meet up with some old friends, and then on to San Francisco. It was there that my carefully planned schedule got derailed.

At a party, I was introduced to Arturo, a Mexican from out of town. He was studying in Tucson, Arizona and I was intrigued by his warm, easy-going energy and engaging personality. We chatted about all manner of things and at the end of the evening he invited me to take a trip to Tucson to visit him. I thanked him for his kind offer, but told him that a trip to the South West USA was not on my itinerary. "I think that surely you are not a slave to your own schedule," he replied, "In life we should be flexible and accept what life brings, no? Who knows what fate God has decided for us? Here's my number, if you decide to come give me a call. Mi casa es su casa!"

And so it was that ten days later I took an unplanned detour.

Tucson is surrounded by mountains - as if sitting in the hollow of a huge crucible. Native Americans consider it a sacred site where the energies of Mother Earth are strong, and it is supposed to be a good place to experience personal transformation. People entering the crucible tend to respond in one of two ways: either they find it hard to settle down and cannot stay or they are drawn in and cannot leave.

Arturo was a great host and introduced me to lots of his Mexican and Hispanic friends. I loved their attitude to life and was fascinated by their values and beliefs. Their emphasis was very much on relationships. "A man may work hard and become a millionaire, but if he has no friends he is poor," said Arturo. The days unfolded in a leisurely way and I never knew ahead of time what we would do, who we would meet or where we would end up. Time slowed and I began to relax and unwind a little. The hot desert environment with its weird and wonderfully shaped cactae was a world away from my life in Germany. My sabbatical was drawing to a close but I knew that it would not be long before I returned to this magical place.

Within six months I had given up my work in Germany, and was living in an old adobe house on the edge of Tucson. A friend of Arturo employed me part time in his small consultancy business and I became acclimatised to a very different pace of life. I hiked in the mountains, explored the canyons and learnt how to respect the desert flora and fauna.

Everything was going well in my new life until I started becoming romantically involved with a series of Arturo's Mexican friends. To my dismay, each relationship followed the same pattern. At first I would be entranced by their laidback approach to life and in awe of their ability to go with the flow. But sooner or later their behaviour would begin to drive me crazy and my judgements would start: "You are never on time." "You are so disorganised." "You keep changing plans." "You waste so much time talking". "You never get jobs done." "You are over-emotional and totally irrational."

I struggled to understand what kept going wrong. Why was I both attracted to and judgemental of these people? Was there something wrong with me? What could I do to change these painful patterns? In my search for answers to these questions I tried many different modalities and techniques - Psychodrama, Rebirthing, Holotropic Breathwork, the Hoffman Quadrinity Process, the Sedona Release Technique.... I read all the latest self-help books and visited counsellors and shamans, tarot readers and astrologers. The heat was on and the crucible would not let me escape. I was by turns grilled, boiled, fried, baked and roasted!

After three intensive years of introspection I was starting to feel burnt out. How could this be? Wasn't this the same feeling I had had in Germany? I had left the intensive seminar circuit behind and yet here I was feeling stressed again! I was on the point of despair when someone recommended a new process called Voice Dialogue. Would this be any different to all the others? I was very sceptical but decided to give it a try.

The facilitator was called Gail and in my first session she spoke to two parts of me - my Pusher and my Organiser. To my amazement I discovered that not only had they been running my life in Germany, but that they had been running it in Tucson as well! It was they who got me involved in so many different therapies, trying this one and that one, and never letting me rest. Along with my Perfectionist and Rational-Mind, they formed a formidable team of *primary selves* whose job was to have me be the best at whatever I did - whether it be management training or personal development.

As I did more sessions and discovered more of my selves it slowly dawned on me that the qualities I was both attracted to and then judged in my Mexican friends and lovers were those of my *disowned* Carefree, Easy-Going, Spontaneous, Emotional and Intuitive selves. Gail explained that it was actually my Pusher et al who were doing the judging. With this new perspective, I could see that my Mexican friends were in fact my teachers, helping me to become aware of my disowned selves. I realised that if I was to break the cycle of burnout and disillusionment I needed to consciously embrace all my many selves, including the more relationship oriented Mexican ones and the more task oriented Germanic ones.

How perfect that Arturo had invited me to Tucson! The crucible had worked its alchemy and could now release me. I left the dry desert of Arizona and moved to the moist coast of California. I had found a new path and taken my first steps on the journey of selves discovery.

In Flight Selves

The theory of the Psychology of Selves says that as we grow up we develop primary selves that keep us safe in the world, protecting our vulnerability. The price we pay is that we more or less disown the opposite selves, and also lose touch with our vulnerability. When we encounter our disowned selves in other people, we either judge them or put them on a pedestal and find them mysteriously attractive. I had an experience of both on a flight to London from San Francisco.

I had booked an aisle seat and, when I boarded, a middle-aged couple were settling in to the two seats next to me on my left - the woman by the window, the man using my seat to unpack things from his bag that he would need during the flight. I said, "Hello". But he didn't acknowledge me and seemed irritated that I had arrived to take my seat before he had finished. As we headed east at 35,000 feet he clearly felt it was his right to use the whole of the armrest and block my reading light by holding his book up high in front of him. He never said, "Excuse me" or "Thank you" when he had to get by to use the toilet. I noticed that he only used monosyllables and grunts to respond to his wife's questions and requests; and, to top it all, he drank quantities of wine and spirits!

You have to understand that my primary selves have to do with being polite, communicative, respectful, accommodating, and pleasant to others. Also, I seldom drink alcohol. So here I was sitting next to a whole bunch of my disowned selves in the form of my fellow passenger!!

I could feel the judgements of my primary selves coursing through my mind and body. I felt myself tightening and sitting more rigidly, waiting for the opportunity to recover the armrest should he move his elbow. Then I paused. I was on my way home from a weeklong intensive training with the creators of Voice Dialogue, Drs Hal and Sidra Stone, at their home in northern California. There had been much sharing and analysis of what is going on when we interact with others in so-called *negative bonding patterns*[3]. I decided to put into practice what I had learnt and experienced during the training.

So I first asked myself if I was unconsciously feeling vulnerable right now. It had been an amazing week during which we had all supported each other as we dived deeply into our individual processes. I was still feeling quite open, sensitive and a little lost as I moved out of the safe environment of the workshop and back into the everyday world. I was sad

---

[3] See Glossary, Appendix 2

to say goodbye to my friends in California and also missing my partner in London as I had been away for three weeks. I hadn't slept well the night before and I was facing a ten-hour flight with the prospect of an eight-hour time change and jetlag when I arrived. Yes, I was feeling vulnerable!

Once I realised this, and that my primary selves were on high alert to try and protect me, I was able to sit with my vulnerability and take more conscious care of myself. As I did this I could feel my judgements about my neighbour melting away. I followed Hal and Sidra's advice to imagine taking a little essence of his energy to see what gift it could bring me. Of course! It was one of my issues that I had been working on during the training: *entitlement*. I was entitled to my space and light, comfort and consideration. I could do more than just cope with my very entitled neighbour, put up with his behaviour, be outwardly nice yet inwardly silently judge him. I could unhook from the negative bonding pattern and assert my rights in a neutral and impersonal way through an *Aware Ego*[4]. I felt very calm about this realisation and my body immediately relaxed.

And then a remarkable thing happened. The energy between us shifted. He moved his elbow away, and for the rest of the flight we shared the use of the armrest. He reclined his seat and held his book lower and I had plenty of light. When the snack tray came around half way through the flight I wanted to take two chocolate bars. But the steward made it clear that we were only allowed to take one each. Noticing this, my neighbour took the bar he was entitled to and then offered it to me! He continued to drink but it didn't bother me any more. We never had a conversation, but once I had embraced my vulnerability and acknowledged the disowned selves that he held for me, the tension between us disappeared and I could relax.

My attention now turned to the other passengers sitting around me.

Across the aisle were a young family - mother, father and between them their little boy who I guessed was probably around three years old. The father was good looking, wearing fashionably relaxed clothing that intimated a defined yet not overly muscular physique. His clothes - designer jeans, a T-shirt with some kind of biker logo on it and black leather boots - suggested a macho personality. Yet in his interactions with his wife, fellow passengers and air stewards he was soft spoken and polite. He also supported and hugged his wife when she appeared overwhelmed with the task of feeding or changing their son. *I imagined him to be a perfect lover.* With his son he was attentive, caring and patient. *The perfect father!* I also noticed that he had strong, powerful hands.

---

[4] See Glossary, Appendix 2

Having resolved my negative bonding with the passenger to my left, I now felt my attention shifting more and more to this *wonderful* man to my right. To me he seemed to embody the essence of strong yet sensitive male energy. I realised that in my fantasy about him I was putting him onto a pedestal and making him too perfect. So what disowned selves were at work here?

On my wall at home I have one of Jan Saudek's iconographic pictures called "Life". It shows a young, muscular, working-class man wearing jeans and no shirt, holding a naked baby to his chest. We cannot see his face or the lower part of his body. His hands are large and his nails are stained, indicating that he does hard manual work. The baby seems secure and safe in his arms - one hand cradling its body, the other protecting its head. The image is immensely strong yet tender and I have always been drawn to it. I imagined my neighbour to be exactly this kind of man.

My grandfather was a blacksmith - strong and with the kind of hands that Saudek's man and my fellow passenger had. He left school when he was fourteen. He wanted me to get the education he never had and go to university. When I accessed his energy inside me many years ago in a Voice Dialogue session with Hal, this introjected self said that he now regretted this because going to university had created a monster! He saw me as effete, overly sophisticated and much too intellectual. His injunction was simple: work hard, eat when hungry and sleep when tired.

As I grew up, I developed a very strong Rational-Mind as a primary self and I have experienced a lot of my life through that Rational-Mind. I have largely disowned my grandfather's hands and his kind of practical, responsible masculinity. I have never had a manual job or taken care of a wife and children. My own strong, nurturing father and husband energies have been buried. I realised I was projecting these disowned selves onto the man to my right.

So what was the lesson here? As I watched this capable father across the aisle I could see that by embracing some of my disowned masculine energy I would have more confidence and presence in the world; I would be more balanced and grounded in my relationships; and, most importantly, I would be better able to nurture and protect my own Inner Child.

The journey seemed to pass more quickly than usual, yet as I disembarked I felt I had travelled much further than the distance between San Francisco and London!

3

CHOOSING BETWEEN OUR SELVES

Whether it's deciding on what clothes to wear, or fighting the temptation to eat that delicious but fattening pastry, the pull of opposite and competing selves can be felt even in the simplest of daily activities. Standing in the space between these selves and holding the tension of opposites brings new and creative responses to life's dilemmas.

Who's Dressing You?

I have a cartoon in front of me. It shows a character in a dressing gown commenting as she looks through her wardrobe, trying to decide what to wear to go to work that day. "Incredible new dress, but I can't find any shoes to go with it.... Ah! Perfect shoes, but no matching skirt.... Hmm. Wonderful skirt, but no matching blouse..... Oh! Great blouse, but no matching slacks, dress, shoes, jewellery or belt...!"

In the final scene she is sitting on the bed phoning her boss: "The individual parts of me are all prepared to come to work Mr Jones, but as a group we won't be able to make it."

I had a similar crisis the other morning getting ready to teach a one-day workshop. At least two different parts were trying to dress me. It was a warm day and I knew the participants would be dressed casually. The atmosphere would be relaxed and everyone would be expecting to have fun. Even so, my Conservative self thought I should wear a newly pressed pair of chinos, polished leather shoes and a smart shirt. As far as that part of me was concerned, a workshop leader should project an image of professionalism. Otherwise my status would be undermined and I wouldn't be taken seriously.

My Conservative self remembers with embarrassment an incident some years ago when I was teaching a one-week seminar in Japan. The participants were all senior managers and I wore a suit and tie every day. Halfway through the week I wanted to get some feedback from my Japanese colleague who had organised the programme. I waited until we were sitting naked in the communal hot bath. For Japanese this is a situation where the requisite Polite and Pleasing selves can be put to one side and one can be open and reveal one's true feelings or *"honne"*.

"So, Jugoro-san, how do you think the seminar is going?" I asked. My own sense was that all was going well, so I was quite taken aback when he hesitated, drew breath and said, "Maybe there is a problem, Kento-san." A problem? What could it be? My mind raced through various possibilities. Perhaps they didn't like the content. Maybe my English was too difficult for them. Or had I inadvertently been culturally insensitive? "Please tell me Jugoro-san, so that I can fix it," I said.

"Well, Kento-san, it's your shirts," he replied. My Shirts?! I didn't understand. I wore a clean, pressed shirt every day. They weren't loud or over-styled. "Please explain," I urged. "You wore a blue shirt on Monday and a red striped one Tuesday and a grey one today. They don't understand why," he answered. Now I was really puzzled. He continued,

"As the "sensei", or teacher, you have to be sincere, calm and consistent in order for them to trust you and receive your teaching. Wearing a different coloured shirt every day is not showing consistency and this is confusing to them."

The lesson was learnt and ever since, my Conservative self has had a heightened sensitivity to my appearance and especially how my clothes might impact a group in a negative way. With this memory in mind the message was clear - I should play safe and not be controversial. I reached for my chinos. But even as I took them out of the cupboard another voice intervened.

It was my Exhibitionist self, a part of me that loves to be provocative. Allied with a Rebel self, this is a part of me that delights in shocking people, and one way to do that is to have me wear unusual or unconventional clothes. He once had me buy a T-shirt that said: "F_CK, all I want is U"! Needless to say, my Conservative self made sure that it languished in a bottom drawer, buried beneath what it considered to be more "decent and respectable" clothing.

One look at the chinos and my Exhibitionist rebelled. No way was he going to let me wear such "non-descript and boring" clothes! As I scanned my wardrobe his eyes settled on a blue T-shirt. Printed in big letters on the front were the words: "Just another sexy bald bloke." That would do nicely. I put it on and then pulled on a pair of Levi's. A brassy cowboy belt and an old pair of trainers and the outfit was complete. I looked in the mirror. He was satisfied.

It wasn't more than a few seconds before the voice of my Conservative self bellowed in my head, "Are you seriously going to stand in front of a group of complete strangers wearing such inappropriate clothing!?" And so the to and fro between these two selves began. I took the jeans and T-shirt off and replaced them with the chinos and shirt. I looked in the mirror. My Exhibitionist gave his frank opinion, "Dull, drab and dreary!!"

Phoning in and cancelling the workshop like the cartoon character was not an option. I needed to sit with these two opposing selves and find a solution. I changed back into my pyjamas and went downstairs to have breakfast. As I sat munching my toast I listened to their arguments. I knew that whatever I chose to wear, one of them would be upset.... Finally, as I sipped the last of my coffee I decided. I went upstairs made my selection, dressed myself and left for the workshop.

So who won? Which self turned up to teach my workshop - my Conservative or my Exhibitionist? With a nod to both I chose to wear the jeans with a conventional belt, the trainers, and a neutral coloured shirt. That way both selves could be present to inform my work. I could be professional _and_ casual. Sitting over breakfast and listening to the voices of both my opposing selves enabled me to take charge of them rather than have either one take charge over me!

The 'war of the wardrobe' can offer wonderful insights both for facilitator and client in a Voice Dialogue session. On one occasion for example, a lady who for several sessions had worn unobtrusive pastel colours, arrived in a bright red dress. That day her Sexual-Rebel spoke out. "Did you dress her this morning," I asked. "You bet!" she said feistily, "It's about time she listened to me!!" Or the tolerant, new-age mother who turned up one day in a dark top with a wide, pristine white collar. Her inner Puritan who railed against her easy going attitude to raising her children wanted _his_ presence to be noted and _his_ voice heard: "Spare the rod and spoil the child!" was his message.

So, take a moment to observe what you are wearing right now and ask yourself, "Who dressed me today?" Maybe this will clue you in to a particular self that is trying to get your attention and appreciation.

Snow Selves

I woke up and flicked the radio on before opening the curtains. "It's the worst snow in London for eighteen years," said the early morning newsman. "All bus services have been suspended, many trains have been cancelled and schools closed." My immediate response was to feel angry that my plans had been disrupted, but before I knew it, I was up and peering through the window, excited to see the thick white blanket of snow muffling the street.

As I gazed outside I felt myself being tugged in two opposing directions. For my more controlling, professional selves the disruption the snow caused was really annoying. I would have to make phone calls to cancel or postpone meetings and change my sacred schedule! On the other side were my younger, more light-hearted selves, happy at the opportunity the snow gave them to come out and play.

If I allowed the former to take control, I knew I would spend the day inside working at my computer and frowning through the window as the snow continued to fall. Come the end of the day, my inner kids would be upset and would make me feel like a real spoilsport for not having let them out. If, on the other hand, I went with the latter, I would use the weather as an excuse to take the day off completely and abandon all thoughts of work. That would incur the judgement of my Pusher and Organiser who would make me feel enormously guilty for "wasting my day".

I knew I would have to sweat this choice - to spend some time holding the tension between these opposing selves - if I was going to make the most of the day and not end up feeling frustrated.

I let these voices battle it out in my head as I had my shower and got dressed. After a hearty breakfast it was time to decide. Putting an arm around both camps I let them know my compromise. I would deal with the phone calls, rescheduling and some emails first, then I would go outside with my partner - who was also unable to get to work - and enjoy the snow while it was daylight. In the late afternoon after dark I would come back to work at my computer again. Sorted.

Or so I thought. How hard it was to stay conscious!

I completed the tasks I had set myself and then, as if on autopilot, found myself writing another email, checking another document and making yet another phone call. The morning was slipping away from me. I heard my Pusher whispering, "Just one more thing, and then go out. Just one...."

And at the same time I became aware of the growing upset on the other side: "Are we going out or not? Are you going to keep your promise?" I closed the computer, called to my partner that I was finally ready, and put on my boots and coat.

Outside was magical - the enveloping white, the crunch of the snow under foot, the lack of traffic, the cold drip down my neck as my partner's snowball hit its mark. Our Inner-Kids came out to play. With schools closed, there were lots of children and teenagers out on the streets having a great time. Some had built a huge snowman with a carrot nose and apples for eyes. Others were pulling each other along on makeshift sledges.

The faces of the adults showed differing reactions and I wondered how many of them had gone through the same inner dialogue as me. Some fathers were obviously delighted to have an unexpected day off with their kids. Couples walked hand in hand smiling and chatting as they sipped warming cups of coffee - for them the weekend had arrived early! However, others betrayed different emotions. Gripped by their fearful selves, older people shuffled along, anxious that they might slip and fall. Frustrated businessmen headed with gritted teeth towards the station just in case a train might arrive and carry them late to work. I could imagine their inner voices sounding: "Bloody snow!" "Another day wasted!" "That's all I need right now!"

When we got to the local supermarket I was surprised to see it was crowded, but there weren't too many smiles. An atmosphere of mild panic hung over the aisles. Then I realised why. There was no milk on the shelves, no eggs, only a few tins of soup, barely any bread and many other basics were in short supply. The daily delivery had not been able to get through. I could feel an anxious part of me starting to kick in, "Quick, we should buy what we can before it all disappears! What will we do if we run out of bread?" Here was the part of me that sees the glass as half empty. Almost immediately another voice responded, "Just chill. This is panic buying. Don't get caught up in it. There's plenty of food at home." I smiled to myself and we left the shop empty handed.

We walked through the winter wonderland lobbing snowballs and shaking trees so that the snow fell from the branches onto our heads. As we arrived home, damp but happy, darkness was descending.

Back at my desk and ready for a good few hours of graft, I reflected on this snowiest day for eighteen years. I thought about how easily external conditions can influence our inner climate. I ran through the cast of inner characters that had showed up in myself and others - the Pusher, the Controller, the Magical-Child, the Fearful self, the frustrated

Businessperson, the Deficit self, the Easy-Going one - and felt thankful that I had sweated the choice and managed (for the most part) to stay conscious.

Sweet Temptation

'The only thing I can't resist is temptation,' wrote Oscar Wilde.

Standing in front of the display of cakes and pastries at Torelli's - my local café - I am sorely tempted. There are butter croissants, pains aux chocolats, frangipanis, pains aux raisins, flapjacks, fairy cakes, jam doughnuts, apple and apricot Danishes, a carrot cake, and a soft cheesecake on a delicious biscuit base.

A voice inside me says, "Don't succumb!", but immediately another voice counters with, "Why not? Just one with your coffee. Start your diet tomorrow. You didn't have one yesterday. You deserve one!" As I stand in line waiting to be served, I am amazed at how imaginative and insistent this part of me is as it tries to persuade me. "Your coffee will taste better with something sweet to go with it. You'll be supporting your local café and helping to pay the salaries of the baristas who count on your custom. You wouldn't want to let them down, would you? It will make them happy if you buy one."

There is an air of desperation about this Sweet-Tooth self - almost as if it is afraid of what will happen if I don't indulge. I can feel the muscles in my stomach tense up. Will I give in…..?

I grew up in a home where there was always a ready supply of homemade cakes and tarts. My mother loved to bake and no teatime was complete without something deliciously sweet on the table - a Victoria sponge cake, strawberry jam tarts, a coffee cake or a fruit cake. And then there were the desserts that rounded off the main meal of the day - rhubarb crumble with custard, lemon meringue pie, sherry trifle with cream, bread and butter pudding…. It was my mother's way of expressing her love, and so long as she continued to provide I felt nurtured and safe. Whether through her influence or because of a genetic predisposition, Sweet-Tooth has exerted a strong influence on my food choices throughout my life.

I know that whenever my normal desire for cakes, pastries and biscuits increases it's a sign that parts of me are feeling anxious or vulnerable. Rather than consciously dealing with whatever it is that's causing these feelings to arise, Sweet-Tooth has me head for the nearest patisserie or put a couple of extra boxes of chocolate biscuits in my basket at the supermarket. The sugar acts as a palliative, a kind of self-nurturing that provides a measure of comfort and a temporary relief from my inner disquiet.

In the past few months, since my partner left for an eight-month stay in his home country of Thailand, my consumption has risen significantly. Of course, he and I are in regular communication via phone, email, Skype and text, but that does not satisfy my need for physical connection and intimacy. I miss him and in an effort to mask the feelings of loneliness and emptiness Sweet-Tooth has made a daily ritual of the trip to Torelli's and its 'irresistible temptations'.

In the last week, however, something has changed. Results from a regular medical check up found that my cholesterol levels are much too high. A consultation with my doctor and an in-depth discussion of my eating habits with a nutritionist pointed to an irrefutable conclusion: I have to give up cakes, pastries and biscuits. Family history makes it imperative - my mother died of a stroke and my father of a heart attack. It is obvious that my health and longevity depend on my ability to change my diet.

So now there is a new voice in my head, a voice I am calling my Aware-Eater. He is there all the time, looking over my shoulder, advising me what to eat and what not. He takes his rules from the nutritionist: cut down on fats, especially saturated fatty acids; and as for hydrogenated fats and trans fatty acids, they are *out* completely! He has me read ingredient and nutrition labels on everything I buy and if I transgress, his friend, my Inner-Critic, gives me an earful!

As I stand wavering in front of the display in Torelli's, it's the voice of my Aware-Eater that is telling me not to succumb, tightening my stomach in resistance. "But if you don't eat something," says Sweet-Tooth, "you'll be overcome with longing for your partner." "Eat the doughnut and you'll die young," counters Aware-Eater. I feel stuck between a rock and a hard place. These selves are at war in me!

Realising that whichever decision I make I am going to upset one of them, I take a deep breath. It's time to place my order. "Which pastry are you having today?" asks Camillo my favourite barista, "Only the coffee today thanks," I reply, "I just found out that I have high cholesterol, so I've decided it is one pastry a week from now on."

As I sit and drink my coffee I congratulate myself on being able to stand between Sweet-Tooth and Aware-Eater and make a conscious choice. I realise that apart from giving me knowledge that may well prolong my life, the result of the blood test offers me an invitation to take more care of my feelings around my partner's absence and to nurture my younger selves in more healthy ways.

Choosing Peppar

We were excited but also a little nervous as we boarded the suburban train. Having spent many months discussing the pros and cons of adopting a dog, my partner and I were finally on our way to look for a new addition to our family!

We were off to Battersea Dogs and Cats Home, a modern facility located behind a huge derelict power station, on a triangle of land between two busy railway lines in South London. Every year, almost twelve thousand lost, abandoned or abused animals pass through its doors and we were hopeful that one of them would be coming home with us that very day.

We approached the reception desk expecting to be welcomed as knights in shining armour riding to the rescue. Instead, we were presented with a long application form which, in addition to our names and address, required us to state our occupations, work hours, income, previous dog-owning experience and reasons for wanting to adopt. We even had to write a description of our house and our neighbourhood. Having filled out the form, and after a considerable wait, we were summoned for an interview where a rather stern lady checked our answers and asked us more questions. Finally, we had to give permission for one of their inspectors to visit us to make sure that our home was suitable.

The excitement that we had left home with that morning had almost completely disappeared and a part of me wanted to rebel against all this bureaucracy and red tape. It wanted to remonstrate, "Why are you making this so difficult? We are here to help you out. Do you want us to take an animal off your hands or not?!" I recognised this as the internalised voice of my father who had a healthy disrespect for any kind of officialdom.

At last we were allowed into the kennels, and almost instantaneously this voice subsided. The dogs were housed along corridors on three floors and as we walked past the individual enclosures they tugged at my heartstrings, inducting my softer, more compassionate self. I was struck by the pure uncomplicated energy that the dogs embodied. They were simply what they were at that moment - happy, curious, sad, shy, cautious, aggressive, hungry.......

I noticed my reactions - how I praised some as "intelligent", "handsome", or "confident", whilst others I judged as being "stupid", "ugly", or "timid". Sometimes my partner and I agreed and sometimes our instant appraisals differed. Of course the words that we used said much more about the qualities that our primary selves valued than they did about the dogs!

After looking at well over a hundred animals and meeting several of them one-on-one, we felt completely overwhelmed. Worse still, we couldn't agree on what characteristics we were looking for. I was attracted to the larger, longhaired variety - especially the ones that seemed alert, intelligent and strong. My partner, on the other hand, was entranced by the smaller, shorthaired dogs with sweet temperaments. With so many conflicting voices in our heads we realised that we needed time to process our reactions, and decided to come back another day.

For a month, we held the tension of these opposing positions as consciously as we could while pondering our choices. Then, hoping that we would find a compromise, we went back. As before, I felt an energetic pull towards some dogs and my partner to others. As much as I wanted us to choose a dog there and then, I was aware of a voice in my head that was saying, "No. Not yet. You are not ready." It felt as if we were being tested. Were we honestly acknowledging the different selves at play in our deliberations? Did we have the patience to sit with the process and sweat the choices? Once again we returned home empty handed and waited for something to stir in us that said, "OK, now you are ready."

Our perseverance was rewarded. On our third visit to Battersea we felt drawn to one particular enclosure. From behind the bars a pair of big brown eyes stared up at us out of a jet-black face. As we peered in, a bushy two-toned tail wagged its greeting as if to say, "There you are at last. It's me you're looking for!" We were taken aback. This wasn't the type of dog either of us had expected. We hadn't imagined that our new dog would be a Rottweiler/Collie cross! But it was too late. She had found us. And that same wise voice in my head said, "Yes, this is the one."

We named her Peppar, and she has settled into our home so well that it's difficult to imagine the time before she arrived. Her interesting genetic mix matches the wonderful pairs of opposites she embodies. She can be both bright and obtuse; eager to please and rebellious. At times she is unbearably sweet and affectionate and at others grumpy and independent. Asleep, she is the picture of relaxation, but when chasing cats or squirrels nothing will distract her razor-sharp focus. Mostly sociable and playful, she can also be fiercely territorial and stand her ground against other dogs.

I know that Peppar has come into my life as my teacher. I watch myself getting into the same positive and negative bonding patterns with her as I have with other pets - she is the child to my Controller, my Strict-Father, my Indulgent-Mother and my Proud-Parent. At the same time, I can also see that all the many aspects that enliven her being are potentially available to me. I've started to practise just hanging out with her, following her lead and resonating whatever energy is running through her in the moment - much as I would when facilitating a client. This is sometimes easy for me - as when she is in a pleasing, playful or relaxed mood - and sometimes difficult - as when her more instinctual and fierce sides take over. In this way, unbeknownst to her, she is helping me to recognise, explore and embrace some of my more disowned selves.

Peppar knows exactly how to be a dog. But of course, she does not *know* that she knows. Much as I marvel at her ability to be totally immersed in the moment, more marvellous still is the potential I have as Homo sapiens to self-reflect, to develop an Aware Ego process that can stand between opposing energies, and as a consequence make more conscious choices.

So welcome Peppar and thanks for being my teacher! I'm so glad we chose you. Or did you choose us?

4

SELVES IN
THE SHADOWS

Popular opinion leads many people to demonise their "dark side" or "shadow selves", suggesting that these parts of us should be locked away, buried and never allowed expression. When we bring these 'in the shadow' selves safely into the light of day and integrate them consciously into our lives, we find they contain great gifts.

Toys R Us

I have no brothers or sisters and as a child spent a lot of time playing on my own. My first playmates were the soft toys given to me by my parents and relatives. Chief among these was my golden haired Teddy Bear, "Teddy", who accompanied me everywhere. He was short and stout and had warm, brown eyes. His paws were made of soft felt and he wore a small woollen jacket that my mother had knitted specially. During the day he was often to be found clutched under my arm, and at night would have to be on the pillow beside me before I would go to sleep. He was my guardian and protector and I felt safe with him by my side.

Teddy's companions were a mixed bunch - a small blue dog, a giraffe, a whiskered cat, a mouse, a grey elephant - to name but a few. One of my aunts was a skilled seamstress and had made several of them herself. They were stuffed with straw or old nylons cut into pieces to fill out their soft limbs and bodies. One in particular had a big impact on me. A caricature of otherness not to be found in a child's play box today, it was a jet-black gollywog. "Golly" had a long body and gangly limbs. Sown onto his head were white saucer eyes with black beady irises and a pair of thick red lips. He was dressed in blue and white striped trousers and a red jacket with a large collar.

Golly was the antithesis of Teddy and from the day of his arrival the soft toys became split into two factions. Teddy led the good guys, while Golly headed up the bad. Teddy's boys were clean, well-presented, smart and polite. Golly's gang contained the louts, the rebels, the dishevelled and the rude. Teddy's team were orderly and thoughtful, Golly's crew rough and physical.

In my playtime, there was often an uneasy standoff between these two camps - a very real tension between them, which I tried to handle by keeping them as far apart as possible. Teddy's squad would be lined up on one side of my bedroom in strict order with Golly's mob lounging on the other. Teddy's attitude was that he was always right and needed to be in charge at all times. His men were law-abiding citizens, on constant vigil against bad and unruly behaviour. As they saw it, their job was to police the ruffians and keep them in check. Golly and his guys chafed under this bit and would tease and taunt across the divide.

Inevitably, when the tension became too much, fighting would erupt and pitched battles would ensue. Toys would stomp on each other, be buried under missiles, be flung across the room or down the stairs. Limbs would be twisted and pulled, heads pounded, bodies pummelled. There would be surprise attacks and counter attacks, with the advantage going first one way then the other. I would become totally immersed in the drama, the epic struggle for good over bad!

Finally there would be a critical moment where, with dead toys from both sides lying strewn around, the outcome would rest on a duel between Teddy and Golly. The pattern was always the same: they would go at each other hammer and tongs with Golly almost overpowering Teddy. But then, just when he seemed on the verge of defeat, Teddy would muster all his strength and beat Golly into submission. Of course, Golly lived to fight another day and all the toys resurrected - ready to do battle the next time tensions reached breaking point.

Our different selves are at war in us. The childhood dramas acted out through my toys were my way of objectifying this inner struggle. Teddy and co held the values of my primary selves that were developing in response to the norms of my family and society. I was to be a good, respectful, clever, neat and orderly little boy. Golly and co represented the parts of me that had to be disowned as a consequence - and they weren't about to be cast into the shadow without a fight!

Two things strike me right now as I write this. First is how easily I can reconnect and identify with the toys on both sides and their clash of wills. I have a visceral sense of being with them once more as I describe them doing battle. Second is the realisation that although Teddy had to win every time, secretly I wished that Golly could sometimes triumph! Now, as then, I feel a sadness that the "bad" guys had to lose and eventually be banished into the shadows.

You won't be surprised to hear that the values of Teddy's team dominated much of my life. They served me very well and allowed me to survive and be successful in the world. At the same time I feel keenly that I missed out on a lot of the juice of life as a result. In recent years as I have worked with the Voice Dialogue process I have been able to invite many of those banished selves back into my life - and they have brought me great gifts. With them by my side I am not so easily intimidated; I can stand my own ground; I have the confidence to stand out, disagree, be different and have the courage of my convictions; I don't have to please all the time; and I worry less about what others think.

In my mind's eye I now see myself scooping the toys of my childhood up into my arms and giving them a big hug. All my toys r me!

The Gift

The small package arrived a week before Christmas. It contained something soft and round. It was addressed to my partner and I, but used only our first names. The postmark was blurred and there was no return address. Unable to control our curiosity we decided to open it straight away.

What emerged was a beautiful, soft toy penguin which now spends most of its time hanging out in the bedroom. We still haven't figured out who sent it, but it is definitely someone who knows about my fascination with penguins.

This newest member of the family joined the penguin clock in the kitchen, the penguin calendar in the office, the penguin soap holder in the bathroom, the penguin alarm clock in the bedroom and various penguin statues large and small that adorn bookshelves and cabinets throughout the house. So what is it with me and penguins?

As a child I had recurring nightmares about being chased by penguins - not just one penguin but a pack of them; and they weren't just any old penguins but big Emperor penguins! In the dream I would be frantically trying to get away as they closed in on me and just as they were about to catch me I would wake up in a panic. They weren't really malicious, just big and overwhelming. I even painted a huge Emperor penguin when I was at primary school. The teacher was so impressed with the magnificent black, white and yellow beast that she pinned it up on the wall for everyone to see.

"Were you taught by nuns?" a friend enquired searching for a possible explanation. Nope. "Did you have picture books about penguins when you were a boy?" Again no. To this day I have no idea from where my unconscious mind got the dream image.

The meaning of the dream remained a puzzle to me until I was forty-two, when I attended my first Voice Dialogue training with Hal and Sidra Stone at their home in northern California. As an optional activity one of the trainers organised a "play with clay" table. As we chatted, she encouraged me to knead a lump of clay and just allow my hands to form whatever shape they wanted. To my amazement what grew in front of me was a very large, erect, phallus! "Don't be embarrassed," she said, "You won't believe how many guys make one of those." I felt reassured but curious as to what it meant.

She suggested that the phallus represented one of my disowned selves and encouraged me to think about the energy that it represented rather than its form. She then invited me to give it voice. As I spoke as the voice of the phallus, rather than something sexual, I found that it represented a confident part of me that was not afraid to show itself; it would have me stand tall in the world and be full blooded, full bodied, physically assertive and powerful; it was creative and proud.

As a child I was very shy. My parents encouraged me to be a good little boy and not to show off or boast. I learnt to embrace the modest, retiring, sensitive energies and shun my prouder, more assertive and physical selves. It was not OK to be big and full and take up space. How perfectly an erect phallus symbolised these disowned energies.

Amazing and enlightening as my clay session was, it was not until the next day that I got my big "aha" moment. Of course! The energy of the selves represented by the phallus was exactly that of the Emperor penguins of my dreams. The tall, proud, confident, erect penguins that had pursued me in my dreams were precisely those parts of me that I had had to disown as a child. What a wonderful physical image my unconscious had given me of my disowned instinctual selves.

Even now my Rational-Mind would suggest all sorts of other interpretations for my Emperor penguins. Their inability to fly might be interpreted as grounded imagination; their ability to survive harsh winters as a sign of endurance; their awkwardness on land and elegance in the sea as an ease with the "ocean of emotion". But I am not seduced by these speculations. Instead, the penguins that share my home help me to connect energetically with their larger cousins - the Emperor penguins of my childhood - and embrace the great gifts they bring me.

The X Factor

"Do you want me to change channels?" asked my partner as I sat down on the sofa. The X Factor is not my preferred choice of evening viewing, and he knows that. But I know that he loves this kind of programme. "No, it's OK, I don't mind watching it if you want to," I replied.

Behind my apparent graciousness, however, lay a long-buried, secret desire. My slightly condescending expression masked the fact that there is a part of me that loves watching amateur performers and finding out which of them has the talent to become a star. It's the same part that can imagine being up there on the stage in front of the judges, backed by vocalists, dancers and a fantastic light show and impressing the audience with a stunning performance. It's the part of me that knows that I have the X factor.

My Performer first appeared when I was a young boy. After Christmas lunch I would take it upon myself to entertain the family with a puppet show. My father constructed a small booth with a stage for which my mother made some curtains with a drawstring. Grandparents, aunts, uncles and cousins gathered round and when everyone was seated and conversation had died down the curtains parted and the entertainment began. I wrote the story, manipulated the puppets and did the voices. I revelled in the attention - and of course the applause when I came forward to take a bow! My extended family was supportive and enthusiastic and my Performer could show off without fear of being rejected.

The world outside my home was a far more dangerous place, however, where people were not always as attentive or approving. After a few hard knocks I quickly realised that my Performer could get me into trouble, exposing my more vulnerable side by laying me open to criticism and even to ridicule. The shame and embarrassment was too much to bear and so he was shut away.

Growing up in London in the 1960's, teenage boys were divided into two camps: those who were fans of the Beatles and those who revered the Rolling Stones. Either you worshipped at the altar of the Fab Four, bought the jacket and got the haircut, or you paid homage at the shrine of the instinctual and irreverent Stones.

I did neither. Instead I distanced myself from these "vulgar" rivalries by immersing myself in modern classical music. While my friends were grooving to the melodies of A Hard Day's Night or rocking to the rhythms of Aftermath, I spent long hours listening to the ballet music of

Stravinsky or the piano concertos of Bartok. Alone with my parents' sound system I grappled with the atonality of Schoenberg and the clashing harmonies of Webern. This kind of music was a mystery to all but a few of my contemporaries and I gained a reputation for being "highbrow" or "intellectual." I wrapped myself in a protective cocoon of "serious" music and as a result I was ignored by both camps. The sensitive child inside felt safe.

Of course there was a price to pay for protecting my vulnerability in this way. I had to further disown my confident, exhibitionist self - my Performer. As I retreated into the obscure world of modern classical music, he was relegated to the realm of my imagination. In my fantasies he would adopt the persona of any one of a number of famous singers. In my mind's eye I strutted the stage with the same sexual bravado as Mick Jagger, wowed the audience with the same charisma as John Lennon, and drummed out rhythms with the same dynamism as Keith Richards or Ringo Star - the very people that my Highbrow self shunned!

My dreams also proved fertile ground. In one I was Mick Jagger. I came out onto the stage in front of a huge audience. The arena was vast and the atmosphere electric. But when I opened my mouth to sing no sound came. I realised that I had a severe throat infection and that I could not perform. I felt impotent and immensely frustrated. I was angry at the infection but there was nothing I could do.

These rock star fantasies have remained with me since adolescence. They get stirred up watching programmes like the X Factor. My Performer knows he is as awesome as Freddie Mercury, as colourful as Elton John and as outrageous as Ozzy Osbourne. He watches with admiration as Tina Turner or Madonna fill a huge stadium with their energy and enthrall thousands with the power of their performance. He wants to be allowed to do the same!

Actually, my Performer does have a partial role in my life. As a seminar leader and trainer I often find myself standing up in front of groups. I even call my way of working with people "entertraining". But when he was recently encouraged to speak in a Voice Dialogue session my Performer said he was unhappy that I was "piddling around" with such small groups. From his point of view I should be up on the big stage commanding much larger audiences. He would really like me to be a mega-star and rock the world!

Sitting on the sofa deep in reflection I watched the X Factor contestants trying their best to impress the judges. Then came a commercial break. The first advert was for some new Xbox software. It showed people singing, playing guitar and drumming to famous rock songs in their home in front of a large Xbox screen. My ears pricked up at the catch phrase: "UNLEASH YOUR INNER ROCKSTAR!!" Was the universe trying to tell me something?

The letter X can signify many things. It can mean secret or hidden - as in the "X Files". It can mean strong or forbidden - as in "X-rated". But it can also represent a magic ingredient or talent - as in the "X factor". And at the end of a letter it denotes a hug. Perhaps it's time for me to embrace my Performer more consciously and, after long years in the shadows, allow his energy to be more present in my life.

My Droog

It was a cold, grey day and I was on my way to see a movie. Having half an hour to spare, I decided to grab a coffee at a local café. One more stamp on my loyalty card and I'd be eligible for a free drink! I paid for a small cappuccino thanked the barista and sat down two tables away from the door. I hung my jacket neatly over the back of the chair, and quietly began to read the latest edition of one of London's free daily newspapers.

I'd only been seated a few minutes when a sturdy woman came in. She had big hair, a formidable bosom, and was wearing a long, flowing coat. She jammed the door wide open and as she swept passed me said, "It is so hot in here! Hope you don't mind." Before I could think, my Nice-Guy had responded, "No problem." I watched her order her *grande* latte. She was being very loud and overwhelmed the poor barista with a torrent of instructions. I noticed that she paid with a £20 note. I decided I didn't like her attitude. Why had I not said "No" to the door being left open?

As she headed towards the table next to me, nearest to the open door, my judgements kicked in *sotto voce*. "She is obviously from a privileged and wealthy background. She is clearly used to bossing people around and getting her own way. She is completely insensitive to the needs of others. She probably walks all over the 'little people' who serve her." I imagined her big house and her poor cleaning lady and the rich husband and the expensive cars and the spoilt children....

She flung her coat carelessly over one chair, put her bag on another and sat down with her back to me on a third. She got a thick book out of her large bag, stretched her legs out and leant back, her expansive hair almost touching my table. She seemed unaware of the space she was taking up and of my presence right behind her. As she turned the pages of her book she twisted her hair distractedly. I imagined dead skin and pulled hairs falling into my coffee.

Even though there was plenty of room in the café, I felt cornered and unable to escape her invasive energy. It was as if she was getting bigger and bigger as I got smaller and smaller. I was starting to feel the chill from the draft coming through the open door, but my Nice-Guy would not allow me to say a word, or even to move to another table. "Don't say anything," he urged, "There's no need to upset her." I felt totally impotent.

As I tried, unsuccessfully, to focus on reading my newspaper, another self started to speak. Behind my mask of composed indifference, its inner commentary entered X-rated territory. My very disowned Mean-and-

Vengeful self wanted to tell this "rich bitch" exactly what he thought. "If it was fresh air you wanted why didn't you get your coffee to go, and sit in the park instead of being so selfish and taking up all this space?! You only think of yourself. You're an arrogant, stuck up cow! Well, I'll show you!!" I fantasised taking her coat and bag and throwing them out onto the street, and pouring her coffee down the drain, or even better over her! Any resistance on her part would be met by force as I pushed and shoved her through the door!! I felt like the skinhead character from Clockwork Orange - a *droog* - the leader of a vicious gang, uncaring and unfeeling, on the attack, out for revenge, ready to torture and humiliate her....

As this fantasy surged, I began to notice my Nice-Guy desperately trying to push back and seize control. Heaven forbid I should act out what Mean-and-Vengeful wanted!

Sitting there, observing these two opposing parts of me I could see that in its own way Mean-and-Vengeful was trying to insulate me from a very uncomfortable feeling of being squashed. I realised that this was in fact an old dynamic going back to my childhood when I had often felt energetically smothered and invaded by my mother. Unable to take my space and stand up to her, I had acted out my frustrations indirectly with my toys, some of which had to endure untold misery, being beaten up or flung down the stairs!

A glance at my watch told me it was time to go or I would be late for the film. As I stood up and put my jacket on I could feel Mean-and-Vengeful urging me to "inadvertently" bump into the woman's table and spill her coffee, but my Nice-Guy would have none of it. I did manage to sneakily close the door behind me in a gesture of defiance and was immediately attacked by my Inner-Critic as he attempted to make me feel ashamed of my "petulant" behaviour.

As I walked to the cinema I reflected on what had just happened and the different selves that had been triggered. Most evident were my primary selves that have me be accommodating, polite, thrifty, unassuming, sensitive, quiet and neat. I had projected onto the woman my disowned selves that have to do with being entitled, asking for and getting what I want, taking my space, and not worrying about what other people may think. My disowned instinctual energies showed up in my fantasy - confrontational, uncaring, vengeful and violent. I wondered if I still needed to go to the movies after living through this rich inner drama!

I arrived half way through the trailers. I had bought my ticket in advance and had reserved a particular seat right in the centre. The cinema was only a third full but when I got to my seat I found it occupied by a woman sitting with her friend. They both feigned ignorance and their body language indicated that they had no intention of moving. A man in the row behind growled at me, "There are plenty of other seats. Why don't you sit somewhere else?" I looked around. All the empty seats were at the sides - not where I wanted to sit.

I felt my Nice-Guy pushing me to say, "Of course, no problem, I'll sit somewhere else." But instead, I took a breath and made a conscious choice to bring in my Entitled self together with an edge of Mean-and-Vengeful. "This is my seat and I would like to sit in it please," I said politely but firmly. My tone of voice made it clear that there would be no arguing. The women gathered up their coats and moved several seats over whispering and tut-tutting.

I sat down, immune to their complaints, put my jacket on the empty seat next to me, leant back and allowed my energy to expand. I was going to really enjoy this movie!

Sexy Beast

Don first emerged briefly and explosively in 1976 in Tokyo. My girlfriend and I were having an argument about a dirty spoon. "OK! OK!!" Jean shouted, "Maybe it was my spoon, but you could have cleaned it for me! You are so selfish and controlling. You never think of me. I always have to do everything for myself!" Yet again I was under attack. I tried to stay cool and behave rationally, but her words had got to me. "For god's sake calm down," I parried, "It's only a spoon. Why do you always need to get so emotional about every little thing!?"

We were both feeling vulnerable. Our relationship was cracking under the strain of having spent eight months together backpacking overland from Europe to Asia. We had hitchhiked from London to Istanbul and then taken local buses and trains across Turkey, Iran, Afghanistan, Pakistan and India. Arriving in south East Asia we had visited Burma, Thailand, Malaysia and Hong Kong before reaching our final destination, Japan.

Amazing as it had been, the heat, the cheap hotels, lack of sleep, unusual food and bouts of sickness had all taken their toll. We were very different personalities. When we first met, these differences had seemed strangely attractive but by the time we arrived in Japan we had become polarised and argumentative. I was identified with control, order, rationality and respect, whereas Jean was a rebel - spontaneous, emotional and assertive. The spoon was merely a lightening rod for the clash of our primary selves.

As the argument geared up I felt backed into a corner. It seemed like I had nowhere to hide. My usually solid defences were incapable of protecting me against her tirade and I felt I was being overwhelmed by the tsunami of her negative energy.

Suddenly something snapped and before I knew it, I grabbed a chair, raised it above my head and threw it at her. "You fucking bitch!!!" It missed and went crashing through a window. Jean screamed and fled into the bathroom, locking the door behind her. I raced after her and, frustrated at not being able to get at her, kicked at the frosted glass panel of the door until it shattered. It was as if I had been taken over by some terrifying spirit.

The sound of Jean's sobs and a loud knocking on the front door brought me back to reality. Alarmed by the shouting and the sound of breaking glass, our downstairs neighbours wanted to know what on earth was happening.

I felt totally ashamed. The voice of my Inner-Critic resounded in my head telling me what a terrible person I was. I felt guilty and contrite. Was that really me? I had never in my life behaved in such a violent way. How could I have done such a thing? It was unforgivable. I felt shell-shocked and exhausted.

I apologised profusely to the neighbours for the disturbance, to the landlord for the damage and of course to Jean for behaving so terribly towards her. It was the beginning of the end of our relationship.

In 2000 the actor Ben Kingsley starred in a film called Sexy Beast. Kingsley had famously won the best actor Oscar in 1983 for his role as Mahatma Ghandi. In Sexy Beast he took on a very different part - a brutal underworld criminal, instinctual, confrontational, and not to be crossed. When I saw the film I was mesmerised by his character. I found him repulsive, but at the same time strangely attractive. His name was Don Logan.

Soon after seeing the film I had a Voice Dialogue session with an experienced facilitator. I spoke at length from a primary part of me that hated arguments. It would rather have me stay in bed all day with the covers pulled over my head than risk confrontation. When I separated from this self and moved back to the central place of the Aware Ego I began to feel a very different energy stirring inside me.

The facilitator invited me to find a place in the room where this energy could best show itself. Without a moment's hesitation I moved my chair to one side and sat bolt upright, legs open and feet planted firmly on the floor. A surge of energy coursed through me. Every muscle in my body felt primed for action. I was focussed and alert. I glared at the facilitator and snarled, "What the fuck do you want?!"

I had become Don Logan.

With deep respect and acceptance, the facilitator allowed this buried part of me to speak. Don was my very disowned killer energy. He hated weakness and was upset at what he considered to be the "soft, effeminate" parts of me that ran my life. They had no backbone and no courage. They were weak and let people walk all over me. If he was in charge there was no way he would ever allow me to be a victim. As he saw it, other people had too much power over me. They needed to be slapped around a bit, put in their place and told what to do! He was fearless and fearsome, intimidating and vicious, and would slaughter anyone who got in his way.

Suddenly I realised what had happened in Tokyo all those years before. It was Don who had come forward to shield me from Jean's attack. I had been so physically and emotionally depleted that my primary selves had lost their grip over me. Don was my last line of defence and had leapt forward out of the shadows, taken me over and had me physically strike out against her. I now understood that in his way he was protecting my vulnerability.

Recently I heard an interview in which Ben Kingsley described how he had approached the role of Don Logan: *"I recognised him and his violent plea to be loved, to be seen and to be embraced… to be let in."* For most of my life I had disowned Don and locked him away. It had taken extreme circumstances for him to break through.

As I have learned to accept and embrace him, his highly confrontational energy has lessened and I have discovered the great gifts that he brings me. With him by my side I am able to set clear boundaries. I can say "No" and people understand that I mean it. He enables me to project physical confidence and courage. In dangerous situations I can bring forward his energy and no one messes with me.

Shortly after the Voice Dialogue session in which Don spoke, I decided to grow a goatee beard. At the next session a couple of weeks later the facilitator commented on my new appearance. "I see you are wearing Don's beard now!" I was shocked. I had forgotten that Ben Kingsley had worn a goatee in the film. I realised that it was Don's way of reminding me that he was around and was not about to be locked away again. As soon as I got home I went to the bathroom and looked in the mirror. "You sexy beast!" I growled.

5

SELF CRITICISM
AND JUDGEMENT

When we point the finger of blame and condemnation at others, there are three fingers pointing back to us. External judgements and inner criticism are two sides of the same coin - both serving to support and enforce the rules of the selves that are running our lives. Listening to them objectively gives us a wealth of information about which selves we are identified with and which we have relegated to the shadows.

Camera Shy

My Inner-Critic was slow to respond but when it did, its attack was devastating: "What a stupid thing to have done! Everyone will see how bad you are. You weren't focussed, you hadn't prepared, you asked leading questions, you were too prescriptive… And anyway, who do you think you are? There are much better and much more experienced people than you. What do you think they will say when they see your lousy performance?!"

That morning six of us had gathered at a studio in central London to make a couple of short videos for YouTube. I would be facilitating two Voice Dialogue sessions that would then be posted on our website and available for all to see on the worldwide web. With the cameras rolling and a small audience to play to, my Presenter - the extrovert part of me that usually takes centre stage when I teach seminars - had taken charge. He had strutted his stuff, delighted to be in the limelight.

But clearly, my Inner-Critic hadn't been impressed. Later that evening, home alone and with time to reflect, he made his views felt. On a private "MeTube" video in my head, he projected every aspect of the demonstrations in minute detail. He zoomed-in, paused, magnified and replayed each perceived mistake as I squirmed with embarrassment. "You were hijacked by that Presenter, but you were not giving a seminar. It was an altogether more dangerous situation. What were you doing exposing yourself to the judgements of others, and making yourself a target for disapproval, ridicule and rejection?! You stuck your head in the air asking the whole world to shoot at you! You know that the only way to stay safe is to keep your head down!"

As I listened to this onslaught I began to recognise the rules of my primary selves - the parts of me that keep me safe in the world: don't show off, stay in control, think things through, and be well prepared. These were rules that I had lived by since my childhood. I realised that my Inner-Critic was simply trying to enforce these rules in order to protect the more vulnerable parts of my personality - my younger Shy and Sensitive selves - and to make sure that I would never expose them in such a way again.

Suddenly I remembered another situation involving a camera. It was twenty years earlier when I was studying Voice Dialogue with my teacher Gail Steuart. I had done a lot of sessions with her and discovered many of my selves. I was aware that whenever I spoke from a different self my body language and facial expression changed. I wanted to see just how different I looked, so I bought a video camera and, with Gail's permission, arranged to film a session.

We set the camera up behind her in the doorway of the consulting room so that it would capture me whether I moved my chair to the left or the right. After a final check to make sure everything was in focus, I switched the camera to record and we began the session.

First she talked to a couple of my very competent primary selves - my Pleaser and my Rational-Mind. They felt comfortable and not at all worried by the presence of the camera pointing at them over Gail's right shoulder. Then a young and tender energy emerged that was very shy. It sat tightly curled on the floor, did not look at Gail and whispered only a few words in answer to her questions. It was very sensitive, anxious about the feelings and opinions of others and afraid of being judged or rejected.

When the session ended we were both excited to see the video. I had clearly gone through some physical changes and was eager to watch my selves in action. While Gail made us some coffee, I rewound the film and switched on the wide screen TV. We took our seats for the show and I pressed "play" on the remote.

I was intrigued to see how as my Pleaser I moved my chair closer to Gail and leant towards her when speaking. My body language was open and my face warm and friendly. I maintained good eye contact and it even seemed like I was playing a little to the camera! As my Rational-Mind I sat further back and was sterner in appearance. My face was tighter and my body language more guarded, arms and legs crossed. Again, I was able to look directly at Gail as well as at the camera.

I couldn't wait to see how I came across as my younger Shy self. I watched as that part of me moved to one side and sat on the floor, but was then astonished to see myself shift back until I disappeared completely from the screen! Gail and I looked at each other in amazement. Neither of us had been conscious of this at the time. I had moved to the corner of the room and curled up out of range of the camera. This was a part of me that really did not want to be seen.

To be on camera, or even worse on an internet video accessible to thousands if not millions of viewers, terrifies my Shy self. On reflection I could understand why my Inner-Critic was so vitriolic in it's condemnation. I had totally disregarded the rules of my primary selves and my Critic's harsh words were an attempt at damage control. To be self-critical is less painful than being criticised by others. It is a form of defence, a kind of pre-emptive strike. If I can say, "I know I wasn't good - I wasn't focussed, I hadn't prepared enough, I asked leading questions, I was too prescriptive," it helps to shield me from the external barbs of those who might judge me.

Now, whenever I sit down to watch myself on video, I invite all my selves to gather around. I put one arm around my Inner-Critic, the other around my Presenter, and place my Shy self safely on my lap. My Critic still has plenty to say. But conscious of the fact that it is simply shining a light on the rules of my primary selves in an effort to protect my more vulnerable parts, I no longer feel knocked off balance by its slaps.

Guilt and Shame

My first impression of the Japanese was that they were a very clean and tidy people. When I arrived in Tokyo in the mid-70's I was amazed to find that there were three rubbish collections a week - two for burnable garbage and one for non-burnable items. Even more amazing was the very neat way households packaged their rubbish. Bags and boxes were tied securely with string and stacked carefully by the roadside the night before collection day. I discovered that people placed great value on the correct appearance of their trash lest they be regarded as messy and disorderly by their neighbours.

My friend and I were in Japan to study a martial art. We didn't have much money and so would go out in the small hours on non-burnable collection days and scavenge for anything we might be able to make use of. It was incredible what we would haul back to our small apartment: a complete dinner set with just one cracked plate, boxed and totally clean; unsoiled pillows and cushions; cups, mugs, bowls, pots and pans; a functioning TV and small electric cooker; pictures, chairs, a desk and bookshelves. Over the course of a couple of months we managed to find most of the basics - plus a few luxuries! We felt a bit guilty about "stealing" people's rubbish, but nobody saw us.

The importance Japanese put on orderliness, cleanliness and social responsibility could be seen everywhere around Tokyo. Public places were patrolled by uniformed workers, each with a long-handled pan and brush ready to scoop up any offending litter that might have been inadvertently dropped. Train platforms were kept so immaculately polished that I felt uncomfortable walking on them with my dirty shoes. In department stores an employee held a cloth against the moving black handrail of the escalator ensuring it stayed spotless and shiny. Taxi drivers, station guards, lift ladies all wore clean white gloves; and if anyone had a cough or cold they covered their mouth with a surgical mask.

My first trip outside Tokyo was to the Izu peninsular, a couple of hours south of the capital by train. I had been hired to teach a couple of residential workshops. The company retreat centre was located half way up the slopes of an extinct volcano outside a picturesque village. It was summer and the weather was warm and sunny. Since I had a free day between workshops I thought it would be nice to explore the area. From a map I could see that there was a footpath that followed the coast for some miles to the next village and I decided to hike it. I set off early with my "*bento*" (a lunch box containing rice, fish and pickled vegetables) and some bottled water, and made my way down to the coast.

The scenery was spectacular. The path wove its way high along rugged cliffs of volcanic rock against which the Pacific Ocean pounded relentlessly. I climbed up across exposed outcrops and down through wooded inlets. I was thoroughly enjoying myself. However, as I got further away from habitation I noticed something that surprised me. The path was strewn with litter! There were old bento boxes and chopsticks, discarded cans and bottles, paper napkins and plastic bags. This ran contrary to my previous experience of the Japanese as being fastidiously neat and tidy. I might have expected this in the UK, but not here in Japan.

When I got back to the centre I told my Japanese colleague what I had seen and asked him if he could explain this contradictory behaviour. His answer (with allowances for the passage of time) intrigued me enough to have stayed with me for nearly thirty-five years.

"Well, Kento-san, from my point of view there are two types of culture in the world. Cultures that use guilt as a way to get people to follow society's rules and behave 'correctly' and cultures that use shame.

"I think you Westerners like to use guilt. You are taught that there is a God who watches you all the time and knows what you are doing. Even when you are alone He can see you. Even when you think bad thoughts He can hear them. Knowing this, you feel guilty anytime you disobey the rules. It is as if He is in your head all the time. Maybe you call this the voice of your 'conscience'.

"We Japanese, along with many S.E. Asian nations, don't believe in a single God like that who can make us conform through guilt. Instead, we do it with shame. For us it is the shame of other members of society seeing us doing wrong, being bad or making mistakes. Being seen and judged by others causes us to lose face and feel ashamed. This shame extends to our family who will by association also feel shame because of our behaviour. This is a very powerful way of controlling a society, influencing behaviour and keeping people in line. For example, rather than saying to her child, 'Don't do that! It's wrong,' like a Western mother would, a Japanese mother might say, 'Don't do that! People can see you.'

"In a big city like Tokyo there are so many people that you will be seen by others all the time. If you drop litter or make a mess then you will be noticed and you will feel ashamed. However, along that remote path by the coast maybe no one can see you. In that situation shame does not operate and since there is no omnipotent God watching you, why not throw the rubbish onto the ground? In time the rain will wash it away and nature will take care of it."

I was reminded of his words recently when walking my dog, Peppar, early one morning. My Respectable and Law-Abiding primary selves know the rule against dogs fouling the pavement. In fact, these parts of me get very indignant and judgemental of other dog owners when I see dog faeces on the street - especially if I have inadvertently trodden in some! On this particular day I was stressed, in a hurry, and it was windy and raining heavily. Of course, Peppar decided she needed to do her business right in the middle of the path, instead of by a tree or in the gutter. I had an umbrella in one hand and the dog lead in the other and a voice in my head said, "Just leave it. You always pick up after her. Just this once won't hurt. The rain will wash it away." It didn't take much persuasion. "Just this once," I agreed, and I allowed Peppar to pull me forward away from her steaming deposit.

Immediately I felt the censure of my Inner-Critic. "You've broken the law, you're two-faced, irresponsible, a bad citizen." I felt the weighty burden of guilt descend on me. I hesitated. Whether or not it was the voice of God, this critical inner voice had certainly grabbed my attention. As I stood there contemplating my crime I heard a single word, heavily laced with sarcasm, shouted from somewhere nearby: "Lovely!!" To my horror there was a workman sheltering from the rain in the cab of his lorry just across the street. He had obviously seen my misdemeanour. Now in addition to guilt I felt the shame of having been seen committing the offence. In an attempt to escape from both the situation and my feelings, I walked quickly on, instinctively hiding my face beneath my umbrella.

When I got home I reflected on what had happened. Painful as my Inner-Critic attack was, it didn't hurt nearly as much as being judged from the outside. The workman's simple jibe had penetrated deeply and struck a very sensitive, core part of me with laser-like accuracy. I could use my Rational-Mind to make excuses and argue myself out of feeling guilty: "I don't break the rules all the time," "This was a one off, special situation," "I was stressed and in a hurry," "Other people allow their dogs to foul the footpath." But the feeling of shame was overwhelming and much harder to mollify.

The late Helen B. Lewis, professor emeritus of psychology at Yale University, made an interesting distinction: *The experience of shame is directly about the self, which is the focus of evaluation. In guilt, the self is not the central object of negative evaluation, but rather the thing done is the focus.'* This would account for shame being a stronger spur towards "right" action and "correct" behaviour as it touches intimately on our feelings of who we are rather than on what we have done.

The "excreta incident" as I like to call it initiated some interesting insights. I already knew about the role of the Inner-Critic in my life and its way of enforcing "appropriate" behaviour by making me feel guilty. What I had not fully appreciated was the power that shame has in motivating me to stay on the "straight and narrow". Touching in to the very sensitive part of me that fears the judgements of others, I could see just how strong a force it has been in shaping my actions and reactions throughout my life.

Looking at my dog lying asleep on the rug I can't help thinking how lucky she is. She will never feel the burden of a guilty conscience or experience the shame of having been seen leaving her poo in a public place!

A Fraud and a Fake

Whilst revelations about Tiger Woods' extra-marital affairs came as something of a shock, the disparity between the image of him as the professional, clean living, sporting hero and the sordid reality was not altogether a surprise. After all, he follows in a long line of upstanding "role models" who have fallen from grace. What was more surprising to me was the degree of righteous indignation that I felt. "His public humiliation serves him right for pretending to be something that he was not," I heard myself say.

I had felt the same on hearing that some of our "honourable" Members of Parliament had abused the public purse with their inflated expense claims, and again when our supposedly fiscally prudent bankers were shown to be reckless and greedy. In each case, there was the sense that these people were frauds and had acted in a duplicitous, devious and unethical way. They had failed to live up to their own professed standards of behaviour.

I was not alone in my condemnation of Tiger Woods, but I knew from the strength of my personal judgements that there must be some buried material that my primary selves did not want me to acknowledge. I sensed that it must have something to do with presenting a professional image that was in some way deceptive. So I decided to do a bit of self-scrutiny.

I had been a management trainer for many years and had made a career out of being "the expert", the one who "knows", who can "explain", who has "the answers". To do this I had developed and honed an amazing Seminar-Leader self who commanded respect and earned me a good living. He exuded honesty and integrity. For support he drew on the resources of a wonderful set of primary selves - my Organiser, my Planner, my Rational-Mind, my Perfectionist, my Performer and my Nice-Guy. With them helping to run the show I felt competent, in charge and in control. Any vulnerability I had was safely hidden from view.

However, beneath my professional persona lurked a gnawing anxiety. A voice in my head whispered, "You're a fraud and a fake, and some day you'll be found out." I had recurring dreams in which I arrived late for a workshop or was standing in front of a group teaching a subject about which I knew nothing or for which I had done no preparation. Sometimes I found myself giving a presentation to an audience totally naked, or having sex in font of everyone and feeling ashamed and embarrassed. In other dreams, the workshop participants were rowdy and would not respect me or even pay me any attention. Often the class contained manipulative and menacing characters I feared were going to attack me. The atmosphere was always chaotic and I felt anxious, alone and very vulnerable.

As I reflected on these dreams I could see that the threatening characters represented aspects of my personality - the unruly parts of me that were lax and ignorant, could dissemble, didn't care about integrity and didn't give a damn what others thought - that I had had to disown in order to identify with my competent and capable Seminar-Leader. My primary selves' worst fear was that these opposite energies would take me over and that my carefully constructed professional world would then fall apart. They fretted that, just as in the dream, I would be publicly exposed and vulnerable.

But was there any basis for this in reality? As I searched my mind for an answer I could feel the resistance of my primary selves. There was something in my past that mirrored Tiger Woods situation that they clearly didn't want me to look at. Every time I felt I was getting close to what it might be, the judgements about Tiger Woods welled up, blocking out the memory. It was easier to point the finger at someone else than to shine the spotlight within. Nevertheless I persevered and suddenly I got it! I knew what the buried material was.

Being a slow reader, books were never a particular passion of mine. The thicker they were and the smaller the print, the less likely I was to plough my way through them. You may therefore be surprised to learn that I left university with a degree in English literature. My best marks were for essays on tomes I had barely scanned. My trick was to read synopses, short critiques and reviews of the set books, canvas the thoughts and opinions of fellow students, and out of this construct my own "original" analysis. I felt a bit of a fraud, but I got my degree!

After university I decided I wanted to get out of the UK and travel. I applied to the British Council and, on the basis of my degree, was hired to work as an English teacher for a kind of anglophile club in Finland. It was run rather haphazardly by local volunteers and I immediately saw an opportunity to restructure the club's activities, improve revenues and increase my income. My Organiser and Planner selves created a graded programme of classes, a comprehensive weekly schedule and a local advertising campaign. People flocked to enrol.

The only problem was that I really didn't know anything about teaching English. Grammar was a mystery to me and I had no idea how to use the phonetic alphabet and teach pronunciation. Someone had recommended a course book, so before each lesson I would frantically read through the teacher's manual then stand in front of the class and wing it. Once again I felt like a fraud, but no one noticed and my salary doubled!

I became a big fish in a small pond and this gave me a certain self-assurance and bravado. From behind my image as the respectable, fresh-faced Englishman - the professional teacher whose integrity, character and knowledge could be trusted and relied upon - an altogether wilder side kicked in. I initiated an affair with a married woman who was a member of the committee that employed me. Had people known, I would have lost my job and quite likely been assailed by an enraged and jealous husband. But there was more. At the same time, I was having another secret liaison with an English teacher working in a nearby town.

As with Tiger Woods, there was an enormous disparity between the appearance and the reality. The only difference between him and me was that I got away with it. I was not found out!

As I acknowledged my own duplicitous, devious and unethical behaviour as a young man, my judgements about Tiger Woods waned. Looking honestly at my own buried selves gave me an appreciation of what he had had to disown in order to present himself as a squeaky clean, super sportsman. How would I have felt if people had realised what I was up to and accused me of being "arrogant", a "fraud" and a "fake"? Although it would have been extremely painful for me, it would not have been an international news story. The lurid details of Tiger Woods' liaisons made media headlines around the world. I empathised with how vulnerable he must be feeling.

Often professionals such as sportsmen, teachers, politicians, bankers, priests, doctors, lawyers and therapists have to hide their vulnerability and bury "unacceptable" parts of their personality in order to maintain their image and status. This earns them kudos and/or cash and keeps them secure. However, sometimes the hold of the primary selves slips and the disowned material breaks through in highly charged and negative ways.

The theory of the Psychology of Selves tells us that if we identify with certain selves and allow them to unconsciously run our lives, of necessity we will disown their opposites. And there is a price to pay. The longer and more deeply we bury them, the more likely they will cause us grief when they show up in our lives. This is especially so with our instinctual energies like our sex drive. Our task is to understand and honour every aspect of what makes us human and to find a conscious balance between all the many competing parts of our psyche.

The Ancient Greeks understood this very well and described it in their mythology. They knew that an offering had to be placed at the altar of every god and goddess. You could have your favourites - for example

Apollo, the god of the mind. But if you left the opposite god out - in this case Dionysius, the god of wine and revelry - it was he that attacked you. It is the disowned energy that kills us - as Tiger Woods has discovered to his cost.

Whilst I don't condone Tiger Woods' behaviour, I am grateful to him. Exploring my initial judgements has allowed me to uncover and integrate some of my selves that have lived in the shadows. As I do this I no longer feel the need to condemn him in such a visceral, holier-than-thou way. As the saying has it, "There, but for the grace of God, go I."

The Seminar Leader

As a Voice Dialogue teacher and facilitator, it is humbling to realise how hard it can be to separate from a powerful primary self and how vigilant we must be least we go unconscious and are taken over by its energy. These selves are like a huge planets - before we know it, we have been drawn into their orbit and captured by their high gravitational pull. I was reminded of this recently while teaching a management seminar in Modena, Italy.

Over the past few years, the poor economic climate has meant that many companies have cut their training budgets. As a result I have been asked to lead seminars alone. Although this has meant working harder, it has made a part of me very happy, as I have not had to take into account the opinions, concerns and needs of a co-trainer. I have been able to do it my way, i.e. the way my Seminar-Leader self likes to do it!

In Modena, however, the Italian client had sufficient funds for two trainers, and once again I was asked to work with a colleague - someone whose style and approach is very different from my own.

I began training when I was just seventeen years old. The wife of my English teacher at high school was the local representative of the European Student Travel Organisation (ESTO). Her job was to find host families and English teachers for groups of French teenagers coming to London on two-week study programmes. One of her teachers had fallen ill and her husband had suggested me as a last minute substitute!

"But I have never stood in front of a class and taught anybody anything," I protested. "I know you have it in you," replied Eric, "It will be a good experience for you - and you will earn a little holiday money too. It will really help Penny out if you can take it on." My Pleaser could not refuse him and with great trepidation I acquiesced.

I can still remember the butterflies in my stomach, my sweaty palms and my pounding heart as I was introduced to the mixed sex class of 25 rowdy youths: "This is Mr Kent, your English teacher," announced Penny. Some were younger than me, but most were my age or older. How was I going to control them, let alone teach them anything? What authority could I possibly have? I felt shy and vulnerable and wished I had never agreed to do this.

There was a moment of silence as they stared at me - a mixture of wariness and expectation on their faces, checking me out to see if I was worthy of their respect. I knew I had to be proactive. I had to seize the initiative.

As I stared back at them, something shifted inside me and to my surprise I suddenly felt suffused with a calm, quiet energy. My mind cleared and in a cool, confident voice I heard myself say, "Good morning everyone. Let's begin the first lesson." My Seminar-Leader self was born.

Eric had been right, I did have it in me. I continued to work with ESTO during my university vacations and when I graduated I followed a career as a trainer. Over the years, my Seminar-Leader grew from strength to strength, learning from each new opportunity and assignment. By the time I was in my late thirties it had become a powerful force in my professional life. Just how dominant - and domineering - it was only became clear to me in the late 1980's when I was teaching cross-cultural communication seminars in the USA.

I met Patricia while studying Voice Dialogue in Tucson, Arizona. She was also a trainer, with some expertise in international business relations. We got along OK and decided that it would be fun to run a workshop together. The marketing, planning and preparation went well, but when it came to delivering the training I found myself becoming highly judgemental of her style.

Sensing that all was not well, and also feeling some negative judgements towards my way of working, Patricia suggested that we do a joint Voice Dialogue session with another facilitator, Rich, to explore what was going on. After explaining the situation to him, we all agreed that I would be facilitated first while Patricia observed.

When Rich asked to speak to the part of me that had something to say about Patricia's way of training, my Seminar-Leader immediately made his presence felt and I moved my chair over to where he wanted to sit.

"Could you tell me how you feel about Patricia as a trainer?" asked Rich.

"There are only three trainers in the world that I respect and she's not one of them!" pronounced my Seminar-Leader in no uncertain terms.

"What exactly upsets you about Patricia's style?" enquired Rich.

"She is too laid back, too wishy-washy, lacks pace and momentum, doesn't work according to the agreed plan, deviates and digresses, seems intimidated by the participants, lacks confidence and, as a result, loses her authority and control over the group. Why John agreed to work with her I'll never know. She's useless!"

Speaking as this self I felt very powerful and self-righteous in my condemnation of Patricia. Quite simply, she should never be allowed to stand up in front of a group again! More judgements followed, delivered with a vehemence that clearly shocked and upset Patricia who was trying her best not to react to my highly opinionated self.

After a while, Rich invited me to separate from my Seminar-Leader and I moved my chair back to centre. Immediately I felt a much younger energy tugging at me and Rich invited this energy to speak. I went over to the opposite side of the room and curled up on the floor with eyes tightly closed.

It was my Shy-Child - the same part of me that had been so nervous and anxious all those years before as I faced my first class of French students. This part of me did not like my Seminar-Leader or the way he behaved when he took me over. "I hate standing up in front of people. Why does John do that kind of work? I don't want to be the centre of attention with everyone looking at me. I'm scared of them. And now I'm scared of Patricia," whispered my Shy Child.

"Why are you scared of Patricia?" asked Rich.

"Because that Seminar-Leader guy has upset her and I'm afraid she is hurt and angry and won't like me any more," came the answer.

Rich spent some time with my Shy Child and then asked me to move back to the centre. I took a moment to experience myself sitting between these two very different energies before finishing my session. It was now my turn to observe as Rich facilitated Patricia.

The first part of her to speak was a very indignant Judgemental Mother that couldn't stand my "overbearing and condescending" Seminar-Leader. She hated the way men treated women as being less important and less able, and railed against the patriarchal attitudes that "pervaded and perverted" society. As she spoke, I felt my Shy-Child cringe at her words. It felt like she was going to annihilate me.

However, when she moved over to the opposite side, a very young Fearful-Child spoke. This self was cowed by the judgements of my Seminar-Leader and felt bruised and humiliated. It turned out that Patricia's father had been a very powerful and domineering man who had always told her that she was no good at anything and would never amount to much. His advice was that she should find a man, settle down and live her life as a loyal housewife and mother. The dismissive tone of my Seminar-Leader reminded her of him.

Listening to the opinions, fears and concerns of our different selves shone a spotlight on the underlying tensions that existed between us. We were able to understand how on a deep level our protective primary selves were interacting in a negative way as they endeavoured to defend our younger, more vulnerable selves. It was clear to me just how identified I had become with my Seminar-Leader and how his judgements of Patricia reflected my own disowned material. My Seminar-Leader was actually terrified that I would lose control and not be able to handle the class. His powerful presence ensured my safety, but had inevitably caused problems in my working relationships with other trainers, especially when they were more easygoing in their approach.

These memories came back to me as I observed my colleague in front of the class in Modena. I heard the voice of my Seminar-Leader formulating a very negative appraisal of her. After ruling the roost for the past few years, having to work with a co-trainer again reminded me just how powerful a presence this primary self can be in my work life. It also gave me the chance to reconnect to my Shy Child who, forty years on, still does not want me to be doing this kind of work.

I reflected how the dance of our selves in relationships of all types - with colleagues and co-workers, as well as with significant others - can act as guide to what we need to acknowledge and embrace in ourselves. As I detached myself from the gravitational pull of my very talented Seminar-Leader and listened once more to the fears of my Shy-Child, I felt the judgements about my colleague fade and found them replaced by feelings of tolerance, empathy and appreciation.

Miss Coombes

Organising seminars and conferences is no big deal for me. I have a bunch of very competent primary selves who are totally up to the task. They know well how to plan, organise, and structure. They make sure that no detail is left to chance and that everything is under my control. So when I assumed responsibility for hosting an international gathering of therapists, these powerful selves immediately swung into action. They helped me assemble a local team of volunteers, find an appropriate venue, set up banking and payment systems, and create a newsletter that kept everyone up to date on developments.

As the event drew nearer, my focus turned to the programme. I felt a strong desire to fix the content as precisely as possible, and so with my highly competent crew of selves behind me, I took the initiative and started to line up a series of presentations, workshops and other activities. I wanted everyone to get the most out of their four days together.

Plans were going well and I was feeling totally on top of things until I received an email from a previous organiser of these events. She was very upset. She made clear her feelings about the programme I was putting in place in no uncertain terms. She wrote that she had a 'huge charge' around what I was doing. She pointed out that the intention of such gatherings was that participants co-create the programme day by day, allowing for spontaneity and the free flow of both personal and group energy. She insisted that it should be a collaborative activity and not something predetermined by me. She informed me that she had already written to members of last year's organising committee about this. Together they would decide how best to deal with me.

It was as if I had been punched in the stomach. I crumpled inside. I felt like a little kid who had upset his teacher and been scolded for bad behaviour. Moreover, she had shared my misdeed with others who would now be collectively passing judgement on me. I felt guilty, exposed and vulnerable. I wanted to flee, to hide...

These were very uncomfortable feelings, and it was not long before a protective voice kicked in to rescue me. "How dare she!!" it screamed in my head. "After all the hard work I've done, this is the thanks I get! I'm the one organising this event, not her. How can an event like this have no structure? Spontaneity will just lead to chaos. I can't just leave things to chance like that. I'm not going to be intimidated by her. I'll bloody well do what I want!"

With this defensive energy in charge I felt powerful and ready to stand my ground and fight. However, as soon as its belligerent voice subsided, the guilty feelings re-surfaced, accompanied by sweaty palms and a churning stomach.

Over the next couple of days I flip-flopped between anxiety and anger. It felt like I was on a ship in a storm, being thrown first one way then the other. I was out of balance and needed to stabilise.

I took a deep breath. What was going on here? Clearly my Organiser, Planner, Pusher and High-Structure selves had been in charge of preparing the event. Unconsciously communicating from these selves, I risked being perceived as a controlling parent. This polarised people - either they acquiesced like obedient children or they went the other way and resisted. In this case, they had provoked a Disapproving and Judgemental Mother who had shown me up in front of the previous committee and had let me know exactly where I had erred. Her slap had stopped me in my tracks and woken me up to the fact that I was very identified with this particular set of primary selves.

With this awareness came the opportunity to notice the parts of me that I was disowning - my Spontaneous, Go-With-The-Flow, Trustful and Collaborative selves. Of course, these were the very selves that many in this particular community of practitioners held as primary! If I could embrace these selves as I continued to create this event I would have more balance, understanding and integrity in my interactions with everyone. The storm passed and I felt my ship steady, rocking gently and confidently in calmer waters.

But there was more for me to learn from this incident. It was not enough for me just to use the reaction of this person as feedback about my primary and disowned selves. To complete the lesson I also needed to feel into, acknowledge and take care of my underlying vulnerability. Why had I felt so devastated by the criticism? What had triggered my belligerent voice and caused it to step in and defend me so vehemently? What was it trying to protect?

As I sat with these questions a memory came to me from my childhood. I was a five year old in my first year at elementary school and we were learning "proper handwriting" - how to form each letter of the alphabet correctly. The class teacher was Miss Coombes - a rather austere, matriarchal figure. We had a special book in which we practiced writing the individual letters again and again as perfectly as possible. This was easy for me. I had already done it at home with my mother. So I took the initiative and started to join all the letters up just as I had seen my parents do when they wrote whole words.

When she saw what I was doing Miss Coombes flew into a rage. How dare I flout her instructions and start to join the letters up without permission! She grabbed my book, held it up for the whole class to see and publicly shamed me. "Look what this stupid, disobedient boy has done!" she exclaimed. The pain of that moment has never left me.

When I received the email ostracising me for taking the initiative in organising the details of the programme it tapped right into this old wound. To be seen to have screwed up in the eyes of all the participants was excruciating.

There is an expression, *"The wound you cannot feel you cannot heal"*. Having reconnected with this old vulnerability my task was to approach the management of the event more consciously. I still relied on the wonderful skills of my primary selves to create a safe environment for everyone. At the same time I needed to make use of the collaborative and spontaneous energies of my disowned selves to allow for the free flow of thoughts, feelings and ideas between participants. And all the while I put one arm around the shy and fearful part of me, taking good care of him and listening to his needs.

So, finally I was thankful for the email. What I first perceived as an attack had turned into an unexpected learning and a wonderful gift!

The Young Cyclist

The young cyclist sped round the corner on the pavement (sidewalk) and nearly hit me. I was startled and then angry and after I had collected myself called after him that he was crazy! I watched indignantly as he carried on without so much as a glance back in my direction. My reactive voices started up as I walked on towards the town centre: "So irresponsible, inconsiderate and rude! He could have at least apologised. Typical of young people these days!"

By the time I had walked to the next major intersection I had calmed down a bit and started to focus on my to-buy list. I waited for the little green man to indicate that I could cross the road safely. I was thinking in which order I should visit the various shops when who should pull up beside me but the same cyclist. He was listening to his i-pod and seemed oblivious to me. I was incensed!

My reactive voices started up again and before I knew what was happening I stepped towards him and tapped him authoritatively on the shoulder. He looked surprised and wary. I launched in. What did he think he was doing riding so dangerously? He had nearly hit me just now. Cyclists should ride their bikes on the road or on cycle lanes, not on the path, which was intended for pedestrians like me.

He reluctantly took an earphone from one ear. "What's your problem?" he scowled. I repeated that he had ridden his bike dangerously and had nearly hit me. "No, I saw you and avoided you. Anyway, I can ride wherever I want." "Have you ever read the Highway Code?" I spluttered. "You can't do just as you please. The rules apply to cyclists just as much as to anyone else."

It was water off a duck's back. He gave me a look of studied indifference. The green man showed and he raced off, this time looking over his shoulder to utter, "Piss off!" I was left feeling outraged and impotent.

I was unable to let go of my judgements about the young cyclist. I felt destabilised and in no mood to do my shopping now. I needed to sit down and get a handle on my reactive voices, so I headed for a favourite coffee shop.

Sitting down with a comforting cup of cappuccino I started to reflect on what had happened and my reactions. What did my visceral judgements tell me about my primary selves? Startled and shocked by nearly being knocked over, I could now see that several selves had jumped into offensive mode to protect my vulnerability: my Responsible self, my Rule

-Follower, and my Considerate self. I developed them all in my youth under the influence of my parents who were kind, responsible, law abiding citizens. These were the selves that were judging this young guy so harshly. In addition, there was the self that has developed since I turned fifty which makes sweeping judgements about "young people these days!"

I smiled as I contemplated the latter and how I had hated it when my father used to say the same about people of my generation. I realised that my father was alive and well and living inside me! But also alive in me were the energies represented by the young cyclist. As I separated from my primary selves I could feel their discomfort as I started to look at the disowned selves the cyclist represented: Rebel, Rule-Breaker, and my Carefree and Assertive selves.

I suddenly remembered my father saying to me in his later, more mellow years that he was worried that I hadn't been rebellious enough as a teenager. In retrospect, he thought it was not healthy to be such a good boy all the time. Well, of course, I had *secretly* rebelled and broken the rules. I had ridden my bike all over London in dangerous, heavy traffic when my mother's rule was that I was supposed to stay only in the safe streets close to our suburban home. I had also ridden on the pedestrian only zones, and *in my fantasies* I had bad mouthed anyone who got in my way or criticised my behaviour!

As I acknowledged this, I felt my judgements about the cyclist ebb away to be replaced by a smile of recognition. To complete the process I decided to reframe my judgements and ask what gifts a small dose of the cyclist's energies could bring me this afternoon. Hmm…. let me see…. yes, greater self-assurance, the confidence to break the rules sometimes, and a sense of fun.

I finished my cappuccino and left the café to get on with my shopping. As I went from shop to shop I realised that I felt calmer and more expanded. I had a spring in my step that wasn't there before. And I noticed the young sales assistants seemed to respond to me with a smile, a lightness, and (was it my imagination?) a wink of recognition!

6

SELF PROTECTION

Each of the selves that watch out for us, do so in their own unique way. One might inhibit potentially embarrassing behaviour; another might ensure everything is under control; while another might continually be on red alert for danger. What is certain, is that they will do whatever it takes to protect our vulnerability and keep us safe.

The Organiser

My partner left last week for an eight-month stay in Thailand. After six years in the UK, he wants to reconnect with his culture, visit his family and study Thai massage. The trip has been planned for at least a year, so I have had plenty of time to get used to the idea that we will be apart for this extended period. However, as the reality of being home alone sets in, I'm feeling vulnerable. I have Peppar my dog to keep me company, but she doesn't quite compensate for his absence.

As the days unfold, I can feel the presence of my primary selves as they circle around me to protect the Little-Boy in me who is missing him. Their job is to keep me from feeling sad and upset. They are an awesome bunch. There's my Rational-Mind, my Pusher, my Pleaser and my Perfectionist, but chief amongst them is my Organiser who came into existence very early in my life.

My mother was an extremely neat and tidy person and one of her major rules was that all my toys had to be put back in their boxes after I had finished playing with them. I might have rebelled against this, but instead chose the path of least resistance and followed her injunction. As a result, I developed my own top-notch Organiser who took a leading place in the pantheon of my primary selves.

In addition to having me follow the household rules, my Organiser became a useful ally in protecting me against the overly possessive and needy feelings that came at me from my mother. I could rely on him to create structures that would defend me against her energy. Each night for example I lined all my soft toys up in exactly the same order along the wall by my bed. They formed a symbolic shield and with them in place I could safely fall asleep.

Later, my Organiser used my electric train set to fashion similar boundaries. On sheets of chipboard that stretched in a large L-shape along two walls of my bedroom, I created a detailed landscape of undulating hills and valleys with miniature trees, a river, fences, and fields with sheep and cows. Cereal packets became high-rise apartments and my matchbox cars travelled along black painted roads. Through this highly organised terrain the railway track weaved its way in a large and irregular loop, passing through tunnels and over bridges.

I would spend hours arranging and modifying this landscape, lost in my self-constructed world. No one was allowed to reorganise, alter or even touch it. This applied to friends and family alike - but especially to my mother who was forbidden even to dust it! Organising objects around me like this became a way for me to create a boundary within which I felt secure when events, situations or people triggered my vulnerability. I felt I was in control and therefore safe.

By the time I was a teenager my Organiser had infiltrated every aspect of my life, influencing how I arranged my books on the shelves, my clothes and all the objects in my cupboards. I loved the preparation for a cycling holiday or camping trip as much as the event itself. My Organiser had me write detailed lists of what to take, check and recheck that everything was in order, and finally pack my bags with great care and attention. As a consequence I became an expert at planning and time management. I even fantasised that one day I would become a great logistics officer in the army or an operations manager in an international company.

Being so identified with my Organiser has been a wonderful asset to me in my work; but inevitably it has meant that I have attracted into my life people who are less organisationally skilled and who don't value order so highly. Friends who come to stay in my neat and tidy home have the uncanny knack of creating instant "mess" with bags, clothes and belongings strewn all over. Many of my lovers have had as one of their primary selves a spontaneous or more laissez-faire self. At the outset this has seemed a rather cute and endearing characteristic. But as soon as stress levels have risen and we have gotten into arguments, my Organiser has rounded on them, judging them as "untidy", "shambolic" and "out of control".

Which brings me to my current partner who of course feels no need to wash and dry the dishes immediately after eating, or put them away in the appropriate cupboard. Nor does he mind leaving shoes, bags, coats, letters, socks, towels, newspapers, hats, gloves, bottles, jars, tubs and tubes lying wherever they happen to land! In contrast to me, he feels comfortable and secure when his environment is haphazard and chaotic. Too much organisation can make him feel constrained and boxed in. It reminds him of his Aunt's house in which he was raised after his parents died. His Aunt was a meticulous person and was always criticising him for being messy and muddled-headed. No matter how hard he tried it was never good enough. So he finally gave up trying.

We realised early on in our relationship that we could learn a lot from each other - him how to be more organised and me how to let go and be more impulsive. We knew that if we didn't do this, we would either end up gritting our teeth and bearing each other's behavior, or get into a vicious cycle of endlessly judging one another. Either way the relationship would be in jeopardy. For my part, I have practiced separating from my Organiser and choosing occasionally to leave the bed unmade, the cushions on the sofa unplumped, the dishes unwashed in the sink overnight or the garden path unswept. I have also embraced the part of me that is comfortable acting without a plan, and found a certain liberation, joy and excitement in his way of handling life.

But now, with my partner gone and the Little-Boy inside me feeling abandoned, I sense my Organiser trying to muscle in to protect me as he always has. He has already hijacked the pad by my bed that I use to note down dreams. He is using it to list the things I *have to* do the next day - like sorting kitchen cupboards, rearranging bookshelves, cleaning out the shed and tidying up the garden. None of these activities are bad, but if I do them unconsciously and allow my Organiser to drive me relentlessly until they are all done, I will not be able to stay in touch with my Little-Boy. Instead, he will get buried beneath a flurry of activity.

My task now is to keep my wonderful Organiser in check and take some time and space to just <u>be</u> with my Little-Boy. Sitting quietly with him and feeling his vulnerability, sadness and upset at the separation, means I will be able to more consciously take care of him and his needs. Doing this will allow me to maintain an authentic connection with my partner when we communicate by phone or via the internet. And it will also pave the way for a sweet reunion later in the year!

Esmeralda

The first time I saw him he was sitting on a small brown suitcase outside Cliff's Variety store in the Castro area of San Francisco. He looked forlorn and anxious, glancing nervously at the faces of the passers-by from beneath a curly nylon wig. His ankle length dress was decorated with a cheap floral motif and buttoned up to his neck. Over this he wore a soiled, brown raincoat. Perched on his head was a small felt hat and on his feet a pair of old trainers. Leaning against the tin cup in front of him was a small sign, hand-written on a piece of torn cardboard: 'Only need another $285.60 for my sex change.'

Over the next few weeks I saw him in several different locations, always dressed in the same clothes, a few coins in the cup and the amount on the sign unchanged. On each occasion, I felt mysteriously affected by the sight of this eccentric character, silently soliciting the help of strangers. I imagined that he had no friends and nowhere to stay and that the suitcase contained all his worldly possessions. He seemed like one of life's victims, downtrodden and destitute. And yet he had a certain dignity about him. Although I had never met him before, I felt I knew him. How could this be?

A few weeks after I had last seen him I visited a friend of mine with whom I regularly traded Voice Dialogue sessions. It was my turn to be facilitated. I had been experiencing anxiety in my stomach and wanted to explore what the cause might be. I wasn't aware of being worried about anything in particular and hoped the session might provide some insight and perhaps some relief from the symptoms.

After checking with my protecting self to make sure it was OK to look at this issue, my friend asked to speak to the part of me that was causing my stomach to churn. I moved my chair over to one side and felt my body tighten and tingle as if all my nerves were on edge. I crossed my legs and began tapping my foot on the ground. The aching in my stomach increased and I rocked backwards and forwards, my arms cradling my belly. I glanced nervously at my friend as if unsure or fearful of her reaction.

"Hello. Do you have a sense of your purpose in John's life?" asked my friend.

"I worry," came the reply.

"What do you worry about?"

"Everything."

"Everything?"

"Yes, no matter how big or small, whether past, present or future. I worry."

"Are you worried now?"

"Of course! I'm worried about this session, and whether he turned the gas off before he came out and locked the door properly, and if he'll get home safely, and whether there is enough food in the fridge for dinner tonight, and if his seminar participants like him or not, and what would happen if he got sick and couldn't work, and what the neighbours will think if he let's the hedge grow too big, and what would happen if he went to pay for something in a shop and there wasn't enough money in his wallet, and….."

As I continued talking and deepened the experience of being my Worrier, I was amazed to realise that I had begun to feel exactly like the guy sitting on his tiny suitcase begging for money! My self-image was of a lonely transvestite, marginalised and anxious, yet at the same time sure of who I was and of my right to be that way. I had the strongest sense that if I looked in a mirror right then, that is who I would see looking back at me. I would be wearing the same tired clothes and have the same expression on my face.

"Well, it's a real pleasure to meet you," continued my friend, "Do you have a name?"

"It's Esmeralda," my Worrier replied. There was a sense of pride in her voice.

"That sounds like a pretty big job you have, Esmeralda. How much of John's energy do you take up?"

"A lot. More than he knows."

"And do you do this 24/7?"

"Yes. But they don't like or appreciate me," Esmeralda whispered.

"Really? Who are they?"

"Those big guys over there that run his life." She pointed to the opposite side of the room. "You know, the one that likes to be in control all the time, the organised one, the planner and their cronies. They think they are so powerful and so perfect! They hate the way I worry about everything all the time. To them I am a nuisance and they look down on me as weak and effeminate. But let me tell you something, it only needs one percent of what I worry about to prove correct and all the worrying will have been worthwhile. I can't tell you how many times I have saved their arses by pointing out something they have overlooked!"

"Does John appreciate the hard work you do?" enquired my friend.

"No. He's so under the sway of that lot that he hardly notices me. So I give him a stomach ache to remind him I'm here."

"What do you need from John?"

"I want him to notice me and to accept me for who I am instead of ignoring me. I have my pride and I have my dignity and I don't like being treated like I am some kind of freak! If he listens to my concerns I can be of great help to him."

My friend thanked Esmeralda and I moved my chair back to the centre and separated from her energy. I took some deep breaths. My stomach ache was gone.

I never saw the guy around town again. Maybe he moved on. Maybe he got enough money to have his sex change. Whatever happened to him, his image and energy resonated with me. Twenty years on, Esmeralda is alive and well. In fact, I can feel her in my stomach right now. She has a long list of worries, but most of all she's worried about revealing herself to you the Reader and what you will think of her!

7

THE SELF BEHIND
THE SYMPTOM

Each of our different selves informs our body and influences how we move and how we feel. This includes symptoms such as headaches, tension, fatigue and dis-ease. Listening to what our selves have to say – their concerns, needs, hopes and fears - can shift and alleviate these symptoms, often with dramatic results.

Body Talk

I woke up and felt a slight twinge in my lower back. There was no obvious reason for it so I concluded that I must have slept awkwardly. I got up gingerly and made two cups of tea - one for myself and one for David, an old friend who was sleeping on a futon I had rolled out on the living room floor of my small flat.

David was sick. He had arrived from the States a couple of days earlier and had immediately come down with a heavy cold. He groaned his thanks for the tea and said that he needed to spend the day in bed. He wanted to make sure that he recovered in time for a seminar he was teaching at the weekend. Around the room his clothes were spewing out of his open suitcase, his papers and laptop covered my dining table, and his used tissues littered the floor.

It was not the best time for him to be visiting. I had recently bought the rights to the loft space and was having it converted. It was going to transform my flat, but right now it was chaos. The builders had tried their best to be considerate, but it had been going on for a week already and the dust and noise was horribly intrusive. Today they were putting in a new staircase and I had been forced to stack a lot of stuff in my bedroom to make space for them. There was no way I was going to be able to relax at home, so I left the flat to David and the workmen and took the train into central London.

As the day wore on, the pain in my back got steadily worse. I tried to ignore it and told myself that it would be better after a good night's sleep. When I got home that evening I found David feeling better and the staircase up to the loft half completed. He was moving to his seminar hotel the next day but asked if he could leave most of his stuff with me over the weekend. Of course I said yes.

When I woke up the next morning the pain was worse and I had difficulty getting out of bed. David left for the seminar hotel and I pottered around and made tea for the workmen. There was dust everywhere. It had filtered under every cupboard door and into every nook and cranny. As the day wore on, the banging and sawing seemed to get louder and louder. By the time the workmen left, my back was hurting so much that I could barely stand up. I feared that if I sat on my sofa to watch TV I might get completely stuck!

The next morning, with the pain no better, I was getting desperate, and thought about taking painkillers or making an appointment to see my doctor. But then my mind wandered to the Voice Dialogue sessions in which I had worked with people's aches and pains to help them find out what might lie behind their symptoms. "Surely you should be trying this with your own pain," said a voice in my head, "Isn't it time for you to walk the walk?!"

I got a pen and paper and gently sat myself down at the table. I drew a rough outline of a body, made a mark where my pain was located and spent a few moments focusing on it. Then, on a clean sheet of paper and with my dominant right hand acting as facilitator, I wrote down a question addressed directly to the pain. "Hello, do you have something you want to say to John?" Taking the pen in my left hand, I waited for an answer. It is not easy writing with your non-dominant hand, but slowly a reply took shape. "I feel cramped," it wrote.

Using my right hand again I asked, "Please tell me more about that feeling." My left hand responded: "There's no space for me. I feel pushed out. First there was David. Now there's all his stuff. There are the workmen walking all over the place every day. It's noisy and dusty and I can't relax!" The dialogue continued for about thirty minutes during which time I found out that this was a five year old part of me that felt upset and overwhelmed. How appropriate that the pain in my back felt like cramp! Finally I asked this Child self what it needed to help it feel better. "A walk in the park, a long bath, and a hot chocolate," it replied.

That afternoon I took a leisurely walk along the river. I took time to notice the plants, the trees and the birds. I sat in a café and drank a large hot chocolate. In the evening I ran a hot bath and had a long soak. To my great relief, when I woke up the next morning the pain had lessened to a dull ache.

At the end of the weekend David came back for a few days before flying home. Once again I had to put up with his stuff strewn over my living room floor, and the continuing noise and dust from the workmen. But now I found that if I took time to tune in to my inner Child, to listen to what it wanted, and - where possible and appropriate - to act on its demands, the pain continued to ease. After a couple of days it was completely gone.

Since then, whenever I feel a slight twinge in my lower back I take note. I stop what I'm doing and ask myself how I might be ignoring or overriding the needs of my Child within. I have learnt to listen better when my body talks and to respect the feedback that it gives me about the current state of my physical and emotional wellbeing.

I still keep painkillers in my cupboard and do have cause to visit my doctor sometimes. But by paying attention to the clues that my body presents and opening up a dialogue with the voices that lie behind my symptoms, I have been able to heal myself in ways that neither pills nor the most astute doctor could.

Just Amble

I tried to ignore it, but the pain in my ankle wouldn't go away. I couldn't recall twisting or injuring it and was at a loss to explain the cause. Around the house I hardly noticed it, but as soon as I walked any distance my ankle began to complain. I found myself limping and tensing the muscles in my leg to compensate.

Eventually I went to see my doctor who diagnosed a pulled ligament and told me to rest my foot as much as possible. That was easy for him to say. I had a dog to walk twice a day! Peppar was just over a year old and full of energy. Every morning and afternoon we'd do a three-mile walk by the river. She would go crazy without the chance to let off steam.

I thought some manipulation might help so I made an appointment with a physiotherapist, but before that I scheduled a Voice Dialogue session with my friend Michael. Since there was no obvious cause for the pain, I wondered whether my body was trying to tell me something.

As Michael began the facilitation, I became aware of a general tightening in my body. It seemed that this might be something interesting to explore, so we decided to talk to the part of me that was causing it. Michael invited me to move my chair a little so that part of me could speak independently. He welcomed it, asked who it was and what purpose it served.

"I'm the Resister," it said. "I put the breaks on. Without me, those other parts would run away with his life."

"What parts are they?" asked Michael.

"Those big powerful guys over there." The Resistor nodded to the other side of the room. "His Controller, his Rational-Mind, his Pleaser, his Organiser, and above all, his Pusher. They are all very headstrong. I have thick steel cables attached to them but it takes a huge amount of energy to rein them in."

"What would happen if you weren't around to keep them in check?" Michael enquired.

"They would completely take him over and would probably end up killing him!" replied the Resistor.

"How much of John's energy does it take to do your job?" asked Michael.

"About ninety percent!" the Resister exclaimed. "Because they are constantly pulling at him, the struggle to anchor them down is never ending. Take his Pusher for example. It tries to infiltrate every aspect of his life. It can't even leave him in peace when he's walking the dog. It sets targets. A certain distance has to be covered in a specific amount of time, so the walk turns into a route march. It also gets him to use the walk to review his dreams from the night before as well as to create a 'to do list' for the day ahead. Every minute has to be productive. It just doesn't let up!"

"That's amazing!" Michael responded. "I'm just wondering whether you have anything to do with the pain in his ankle."

"Of course I do. It's a result of me digging my heels in, attempting to slow that Pusher down."

"I see. So you're trying to get him to walk more slowly?"

"Exactly. He has been striding out like a man possessed. He needs to get that Pusher off his back and relax. He could use the time to enjoy the river and the wildlife. He should just amble."

Two days later with the words of my Resistor fresh in my mind I had my appointment with Euan the physiotherapist. He examined my ankle and confirmed that I had indeed pulled a ligament and now had some secondary problems as a result of walking awkwardly.

"I have no idea how I could have done it," I said.

"It could be repetitive strain", said Euan. "Have you done a lot of walking recently?"

"As a matter of fact I have," I replied, "Ever since we got our new dog".

"Do you walk on a smooth or uneven surface?" he enquired.

"On the towpath, which is mostly uneven."

"I see. Show me how you walk."

I strode around the consulting room.

"How long do you walk the dog every day?"

"In total about ninety minutes, maybe more."

"Well, I'd say that doing that on an uneven surface is the cause of your problem."

"So should I stop walking and rest my ankle?" I asked hesitantly.

His answer gave me goose bumps. "Not at all," he said. "You should keep on moving your foot or else your ankle will seize up. But instead of striding out like that, just amble."

Like all dogs, Peppar is a very sensitive being and picks up on small changes in my energy. She is also a very fast learner. I quickly taught her to sit, stay, come and drop. To my great frustration, the one discipline she didn't master was to walk to heel on the lead. No matter how many times I pulled her back and said "Peppar, heel!" she always tried to forge ahead.

It was only when I followed Euan's advice to amble rather than to stride that I understood why. For the nearly nine months I'd been walking Peppar, my verbal command to "heel" had contradicted the non-verbal energy of my Pusher, which for her was actually signaling, "Go, go, go!"

Since that day I have practiced separating from my Pusher during our walks and consciously accessed my calmer, more relaxed selves. The result has been a double triumph. Peppar has started to walk to heel, and thankfully, my ankle has healed.

The learning for me from this experience is not to underestimate the power of my Pusher. As one of a group of seriously powerful primary selves it has played a crucial role in most of what I have achieved in my life - and continues to do so. However, as I grow older I have to get into a different relationship with it or the impact of its relentless energy on my body will cause me ever more problems.

As I reflect on this, I am reminded of the advice my grandfather gave about how to get things done without "overdoing it" and becoming stressed out. "Make haste slowly!" he would say with a knowing smile and a twinkle in his eye.

Or in the words of my Resister and of Euan, "Just amble."

Michael's Eyes

My friend Michael was hurting. We were having a drink in a bar downtown. "I am sick and tired of this!" he grumbled, "I don't understand why it won't clear up. Why can't I find a cure?" For months now he'd had an irritation in both eyes. Every time I saw him he complained about how debilitating it was and how annoyed he was that he couldn't fix it.

Michael was a medical doctor and a psychiatrist and had his own private practice. He was very skilled at helping clients with their physical and emotional problems. People would even come to him from out of state to seek his advice. But nothing he did could make his own eye infection go away and he was feeling deeply frustrated and angry with himself.

"I'm at my wits ends," he moaned, "I just can't figure out what's wrong. I have tried all sorts of medication, but nothing will shift it. I'm a doctor for god's sake. I should be able to heal myself!"

Although I empathised with him, I had grown tired of his whining. I decided to be proactive. "How about talking to your eyes?" I suggested. Michael had studied Voice Dialogue with me and was familiar with the psychology of selves. "I guess we could schedule a session sometime," he replied warily. I knew that 'sometime' meant 'never' and resolved to grab the bull by the horns. "I mean right now," I insisted. "What, here in this bar!?" "Yes."

There was hubbub all around us - the clinking of glasses, music playing, people laughing and chatting. I knew that this wasn't the most appropriate location but intuitively I felt that now was the moment to act.

"Move over a little and let me speak to your eyes," I said firmly.

A little taken by surprise, Michael slid his chair to his left.

"Hello, am I speaking to Michael's eyes?"

"Yes."

"I understand that you haven't been very well recently and that Michael hasn't been able to do anything to heal you."

"That's right."

"Can you explain what this infection is about and what Michael can do to help you?"

"That's easy. He needs to cry."

"Really? He doesn't cry?"

"No."

"Is there something that he needs to cry about?"

"Of course! He didn't cry when his father died. His mother died two years ago and he didn't cry. His partner died last year and he didn't cry. He needs to cry!"

"I see. And if he cries then the infection will go away?"

"Yes."

"Is there anything else Michael needs to do?"

"No. He just needs to allow tears to flow through me. Then I will be OK."

"Thank you for talking to me."

Michael moved his chair back and sat opposite me with a stunned look on his face. This short, to the point interaction had taken both of us by surprise. "It's true," said Michael thoughtfully, "I have never really grieved their deaths and I have certainly never cried for them. I've been too busy taking care of other people and their needs. I've never allowed myself the luxury of letting my own feelings out."

Some weeks later Michael called me to say that he had been taking some time out from his busy doctor's schedule to sit quietly and feel the sadness of his bereavements. As he had done so, the tears had flowed and sure enough his eye infection had slowly cleared.

At the end of that year we met for dinner. I was leaving town and moving to another city and Michael had invited me for a farewell meal in a local restaurant. He seemed more relaxed and less driven than previously. He told me that he now saw the eye irritation not as a curse but as a gift. Realising what lay behind the infection had led him to re-evaluate his life. He had cut down on his workload and was spending much more time at home cooking, gardening, walking his dog and simply being with his feelings.

At the end of the evening we embraced and said our goodbyes, and as we parted I was moved to see that Michael had tears in his eyes.

8

THE DANCE
OF SELVES

Relationship demands movement and change. If there is inertia, it leads to stagnation, frustration and anger. Embracing all the selves that want to have their say in a relationship can be challenging but also incredibly fulfilling, offering depth, intimacy and never ending opportunities to grow and strengthen our connection - whether with family, friends and colleagues, or with our chosen partner.

Montezuma's Revenge

My parents met when they were still at school and became teenage sweethearts. At my mother's insistence, they married when my father was called up to join the army in 1940. After a brief two-day honeymoon at my uncle's house in suburban London, my father sailed off to fight in North Africa. Narrowly missing capture by Rommel's troops, he was posted to India where he spent the rest of the war on internal duty. My mother endured the blitz and worked first as the manageress of a laundry and then as a supervisor in a factory that made guns. My parents didn't see each other for five years.

After being demobbed my father went back to his old job in the office of a builder's merchant. They bought a small home and my mother stopped work to become a housewife and later a mother. Life settled into a comforting routine. It was a typical relationship of that generation. My father was the breadwinner. He handled the money and gave his wife her "house keeping" every month. He dealt with the bills, the bank, the house, the car and generally fronted the external world. She handled the baby, the shopping, the cooking, the cleaning and the organisation of the home.

I never saw them have an argument. Their motto seemed to be "don't rock the boat." In Voice Dialogue terms they stayed in a positive bonding pattern[5]. Dad was the generous, providing father to my mum's grateful daughter, whilst mum was the caring, nurturing mother to dad's adoring son. In this way they both took care of each other's inner kids. Life was predictable and secure and they avoided any upsets that might threaten the relationship. But there was a price to pay.

As a child dad would tell me bedtime stories of his adventures and experiences during the war. They were vivid and exciting and I loved them. Mum would tell me of what had happened during the blitz and how a bomb had landed near her house and how everyone had pulled together and helped each other out. I noticed how they seemed to come alive when speaking of that time of their lives. Where had that aliveness gone twenty years on?

Part of my teenage rebellion was against what I felt to be the airless, stifling atmosphere of home. I wanted to breath and expand and break out of their now routine, two dimensional world. When I was sixteen dad said something that gave me a glimpse of what he had sacrificed to

---

[5] See Glossary Appendix 2

maintain their relationship: "Travel while you are young son. You will have so many responsibilities when you grow up - a job, a wife and children. See the world while you can." I sensed a sadness in his voice, as if a part of him had been cut off and buried. I felt that he empathised with my feelings of wanting to escape the confines of their neat terraced house.

And so I travelled. As a student I hitch-hiked around Europe, and later I did the "hippie trail" overland from Istanbul to India and down into S.E. Asia. I lived and worked in foreign countries far away from home. Dad was always excited and interested to hear about my experiences. Mum worried about me. She did not like travel. I came to understand that in order to maintain the positive bonding pattern and keep their relationship on an "even keel," my dad had to hold back his Adventurer self - the part that had been so primary during his army days. It was just too threatening to mum.

For many years I blamed her for holding him back and saw her as responsible for locking him into a relationship that was nice and safe and secure but with little spark or vibrancy. But of course it always takes two to tango and it was not until they were in their seventies that I saw the other side of the story.

After many attempts and much cajoling, dad and I finally persuaded mum to take a trip to visit me in Tucson, Arizona where I was living and working. She had been worried about the flight, whether she would like the food in the USA, whether she would be able to find a toilet when she needed it, what she would find to talk about with people, and a hundred and one other things. But finally she had relented.

For the first few days, I drove them around sightseeing. Dad sat in the front of the car with the maps and guidebooks, mum sat in the back quietly gazing out of the widow. Being so near Mexico dad said he would like to do a day trip to the border town of Nogales and experience something different. His Adventurer was definitely in charge now and mum seemed unable to hold him back. She anxiously acquiesced. We drove down, spent the morning looking around the many souvenir shops and then had lunch in a local restaurant. We all ate the same thing - chicken enchiladas with rice and refried beans.

Later that evening dad started to have stomach pains. They got progressively worse and he ended up spending a good portion of the night on the toilet. In the morning he looked pale and drawn. I contacted a friend who was a doctor and he wrote out a prescription and advised plenty of liquids and to stay in bed. Mum and I were both fine. What to do about our plans for the next few days? I expected her to go into a state of high anxiety and insist on staying with dad and taking care of him. How wrong I was! To my amazement she said, "Your dad is such a grouch when he is ill. It's best just to leave him on his own. Let's go out as planned."

My friend Carlos came by and picked us up and as we left dad moaned, "Don't worry, I'll be fine," in a 'poor me' kind of way. Off we went, me in the front and mum in the back with Bill - a tall, elegant friend of Carlos from New York. I could hardly believe my ears as mum confidently engaged in conversation with him. He was very charming, and I swear it felt like she was flirting with him! We visited some local beauty spots and were introduced to more of Carlos' friends along the way. Each time mum was outgoing and engaging. Over a long lunch she started telling jokes and got the giggles. I was astonished!

We came back to the apartment that evening to find dad still in bed and watching TV. "How was your day?" he groaned. "Oh, it was wonderful. I had a marvellous time. Bill is so handsome and has such beautiful hands," answered mum enthusiastically, "We met lots of people and it was so much fun!" She looked at least ten years younger and was grinning from ear to ear.

And so it went on for a few more days - dad languishing in the apartment while mum and I went out and about having fun. For the first time I could see what parts she had buried in order to make the marriage work. Thanks to Montezuma's revenge her sensuous, confident and fun-loving self had the chance to emerge. Just as dad's Adventurer was threatening to her, so my mother's out-going, flirtatious Aphrodite was too scary for him. It would upset the applecart.

Over the next week I saw the status quo slowly return. As dad grew stronger he regained his authority and control. And as this happened I saw mum shrink back into her dependent role, once more sitting quietly in the back seat and worrying. I felt sad for them both.

My parents were married for fifty-two years and in their terms they had a happy life together, but I could see the price they both paid for restricting the number of selves that showed up in their relationship. I wondered how much richer their lives might have been if the Adventurer and Aphrodite had been allowed out.

E-motion

It had snowed heavily all night and six year old Matt was excited. As he left for school he made us promise that we would take him tobogganing in the afternoon. We picked him up at 2pm and headed straight for the park.

His mother, Kathy, and I had met in the late 1970's in Tokyo where we both taught English at a language school. After returning to the USA she had met and married Bill and settled with him in a suburb of Denver, Colorado. I was visiting the family for a couple of days. I hadn't seen Kathy for some years and this was the first time I had met their only child, Matt.

"Hurry up Mom!" shouted Matt as we parked the car. Kathy got the bright red plastic sledge out of the trunk and handed it to him. He grabbed it and ran off to join some of his friends who were already racing down the slope, laughing and screaming with delight. Kathy and I watched the children from the top of the slope and chatted.

After about an hour Kathy looked at her watch. "Time to go home Matt!" she called. Matt looked up in dismay, "But I don't want to go home yet."

"I understand Matt," Kathy responded, "I can see that you are having so much fun. You can slide down one more time but then we need to go home."

Down he went, staying a little longer at the bottom this time before climbing back up to us. "OK, let's go," said Kathy.

"But I don't want to go now," objected Matt.

"I know Matt. But you see, John is here and Dad will be coming home from work soon and I need to go home and prepare dinner for us all," reasoned Kathy.

"I don't want to go!" shouted Matt.

I wondered how Kathy would handle the situation and how this clash of wills would play out.

"Well, Matt, if I was having fun and my Mom told me I had to stop and go home, I guess a part of me would be pretty upset too," she said calmly, "So I understand how you are feeling. And we are going home."

"I hate you!" exclaimed Matt.

I flinched. Had I ever said such a thing to my parents I would definitely have received a clip round the ear accompanied by an injunction such as, "Don't you dare tell me you hate me!"

Kathy's reaction was calm yet firm. "It's OK that you hate me Matt. I know that a part of you is really mad with me right now. And we're going home."

We got into the car - Matt sulking in the back seat, Kathy remaining composed and unfazed. When we reached the house Matt ran off into his room and slammed the door. Kathy and I went into the kitchen and continued chatting as we peeled vegetables.

After about ten minutes, the kitchen door burst open and Matt came rushing in, ran up to Kathy and her gave a big hug. "I love you Mom!" he said.

"I love you too Matt," replied Kathy.

I was so impressed. Kathy had managed both to accept Matt's feelings and at the same time to set a clear boundary around his behaviour. Because she had honoured and validated those feelings Matt had not needed to suppress them. This allowed his anger to move through, and after a little while he found that he still loved his Mom. Furthermore, by saying, "a part of me would be pretty upset," and, "a part of you is really mad," she let Matt know that he was made up of different selves with different feelings. She did not lock him into a singularity. This made it OK for him to feel both love and hate.

I once heard someone say that emotion is energy in motion (e-motion). If as parents we judge certain emotions as wrong or bad, blocking their natural flow, we encourage our children to develop a kind of garbage dump of the psyche into which these unaccepted energies are thrown. Here they can surreptitiously stagnate and fester - the garbage dump becoming the breeding ground of the disowned selves.

Matt recently paid me a visit at my home in London. Now in his early tewenties he was backpacking around Europe on his own. Although still young, I found him to be a very self-aware and balanced person. I told him the story of what happened on that snowy day in Denver. He had no memory of it but smiled warmly and said, "Yeah, I guess I lucked out having such a great Mom."

9

SELF DETACHMENT

The selves that run our lives when we are young, demand stamina, physical strength and mental agility. As we age, and our minds and bodies struggle to keep up with their demands, it's all too easy to become frustrated and self-critical. Separating from these primary selves, with deep appreciation for the role they have played over many years, brings both calm detachment and quiet wisdom.

Graceful Ageing

Seeing me standing on the crowded tube train, a young woman stood up and offered me her seat. I felt shocked and a little upset. It seemed like only yesterday that I would have done the same for a senior citizen. Did I really look so old? A voice in my head said that I was quite capable of standing the next ten stops to my destination and that I should refuse. If I had allowed it to speak there would definitely have been an edge of indignation to it. I hesitated. Actually, my legs were aching a little and I was feeling tired. I smiled at the young woman and, with some relief, sheepishly accepted her kind offer and sat down.

I was twenty-five for many years. Then when I turned fifty I decided to act my age and became thirty-five! Now as my sixtieth year draws ever closer I fear my grip on thirty-five is weakening. Several things have recently conspired to undermine the confidence I have had in my mental and physical capabilities…..

"I didn't know you smoked!" I said as Karin sat down to eat her lunch, placing an unlit cigarette in readiness on the table beside her plate. Karin is the young Columbian waitress at my local café. "Yes, you knew," she replied with a warm smile, "You said exactly the same thing a couple of weeks ago when we sat at this very table!" Was I losing my mind? I had always had an impeccable memory. I was mortified.

My friend had parked her car in my street to save money. As a resident I have parking permits for visitors for just £1 per day. But when I placed the permit on her dashboard I forgot to scratch off the box showing the applicable time of day. The result was a £30 fine! I berated myself for being so stupid? Me, the Careful-Planner! Mr Organised!! I never used to make silly mistakes like that.

As a dynamic seminar leader I used to pride myself on my stamina. I would push myself and the participants hard during the intensive sixteen-hour days, often being the last to leave the hotel bar at night. I worked longer and harder than any other trainer and despised those who weren't able to keep up with me. These days, if I am to function well the next day, I have to pace myself and make sure I get to bed early. Part of me feels deeply embarrassed by this. It feels that I should be able to work just as hard as before.

The words of T.S. Eliot's Prufrock come to my mind: *'I grow old… I grow old… I shall wear the bottoms of my trousers rolled.'* They remind me of my grandfather who, when on holiday by the seaside, would stroll barefoot along the shoreline arm in arm with my grandmother. When I look in the mirror these days I see more and more of him in my face and body. "And what's wrong with that?" you may ask. Well, it depends through whose eyes I'm looking.

If I look at my current mental and physical capacities through the eyes of the primary selves that ran my life in my twenties and thirties they will find much to judge. My Mind will have anxiety attacks when I misremember or forget information. My Perfectionist will cringe when I make mistakes. My Organiser and Planner will go ballistic when I can't find something, screw up a schedule or double book an appointment. My Pusher will despair when I tire more easily and don't have the energy to finish a task quickly enough. If I remain identified with these selves as I grow older, my Inner-Critic will have plenty of rods with which to beat me! Growing old will be a painful and dispiriting experience.

To avoid this requires that I unhook from the primary selves that have run so much of my adult life and take a little of the medicine of their opposites. I have to allow myself to accept offers of help from others, not remember everything perfectly, not know it all, make mistakes, be more spontaneous and flexible, and take breaks and naps. The reality is that my neurons are not firing as they once did and my body doesn't have the strength and endurance it had when I was younger. To try and pretend otherwise - to still identify with the rules of my primary selves - will only result in increasing frustration and hardship.

When my friend who left her car in my street came to collect it I told her about my mistake with the parking permit. Rather than be upset, she empathised with me and then told me what had happened to her that very morning. She had stayed at her brother's house overnight and had put the kettle on to make herself a cup of tea. Smelling burning plastic she rushed back into the kitchen only to find that she had put the electric kettle onto the gas hob to heat!! We both burst into laughter and suddenly everything lightened up. We agreed that incidents like this would only get more frequent as we grew older and that to chastise ourselves served no purpose. Then suddenly we had a great idea: why not set up a contingency fund to cover the cost of parking fines, new electric kettles and the like?!

Being able to separate from our primary selves and embrace their opposites makes us more compassionate - both to ourselves and to others. This is one of the great gifts inherent in growing old, and the secret of graceful ageing.

Nothing At All

My first job after leaving university had been in Jyväskylä a small town in the centre of Finland. I had arrived in the middle of September to find Autumn well underway in this land of forests and lakes. I had grown up in the urban sprawl of London and the spectacular displays of red, yellow and orange leaves had dazzled and amazed me.

Now after an absence of twelve years I was back visiting friends. There was so much to tell them - my travels around the world, the different jobs I had done, relationships begun and ended. My Finnish friends were particularly interested to hear about the three years I had spent living and working in Japan - a strange and exotic country to them. While there I had begun studying a martial art, which had its roots in esoteric Buddhism, and it was something I still practiced. To my friends my life seemed as rich and varied as the colours of Autumn.

Coming down to breakfast one morning I found a letter waiting for me. It had been posted to my London address from Massachusetts and had then been forwarded on to friends in Helsinki who had redirected it to me here in Jyväskylä. It had been on quite a journey! I could feel something solid inside the thick brown manilla envelope. What could it be and who had sent it?

To my astonishment, when I opened it I found a sheet of paper carefully folded around a red maple leaf and a piece of birch bark. On the paper was written a simple message: 'So impressed by Fall in New England. Ito'. Ito-sensei was one of my Japanese martial arts teachers with whom I had a close connection. I looked carefully at the bark and realised that written in red ink in one corner were some Japanese characters (kanji). I had never learnt to read Japanese and was mystified. What did they mean and what was Ito-sensei trying to tell me? How on earth was I going to get it translated here in the middle of Finland? I guessed I would have to wait till I got back to London where I could ask a Japanese friend to decipher it for me.

Later that same day as I strolled down Jyväskylä's main shopping street I was amazed to see an Asian face walking straight towards me. As we got closer I realised that the young man looked like he might be Japanese! I approached him eagerly. "Excuse me. Do you speak English? Are you Japanese?" He looked startled. He must have thought that I was a street salesman or a religious evangelist. "Yes, I am Japanese and I speak a little English," he replied. I explained that I had just received a short note - just six kanji - from a Japanese friend and wondered if he would mind translating it for me. Once he understood that that was all I wanted he visibly relaxed and graciously agreed to meet later that afternoon in a local café.

Over a coffee and Finnish pastry I found out that he was an exchange student staying with a local family and had been in Finland for just a week. He was interested to hear that I had lived in Japan. The necessary pleasantries completed, I felt the moment was right to show him the script. I carefully took the bark out of the envelope and pointed to the kanji nestled in the corner.

As he read them, first a frown and then a smile passed over his face. "This is a Buddhist saying," he said. "Mu ichi butsu. Mu zin zou." I waited for the translation. "It means: 'Nothing at all. Limitless potential, or everything beyond measure'. I think the man who wrote this must be your sensei, your teacher." I explained who Ito-sensei was. "He must like you to send you this small gift with such a big meaning," he replied.

That was twenty-five years ago. I have carefully kept the leaf and the bark and they now hang in a frame on a wall of my home in London. From time to time something will happen that reminds me of Ito-sensei's gift and I am drawn to meditate on the message he sent me. So it was just the other day when I was listening to one of Hal and Sidra's CD's. The interviewer was wondering whether it was ever possible to find out precisely who we are and whether there is an 'ultimate self'. This is what Sidra replied:

'It's not always a question of who you are, but it's who you are not that we seem to work with… a constant refining of what we aren't. The beautiful thing about all this is that we are none of these selves… but we are all of them… This gives us a richness and a breadth that is extraordinarily exciting.'

10

CONCLUSION

On Birth, Death and Vulnerability

I was raised in the Church of England. My father was the organist and choirmaster of our parish church and my mother was active in various church clubs. I went to Sunday School every week and from the age of seven was in the choir, which meant attending two services every Sunday and singing at weddings on Saturdays (I have seen more brides walk down the aisle than I care to remember!)

I was taught the story of Jesus and celebrated the two most important events in the Christian calendar - Christmas and Easter - every year till I was sixteen. That was when my parents allowed me to decide whether I wanted to stay in the church or not. I left and have not returned. However, many years later, becoming familiar with the theory and practice of Voice Dialogue has given me a new insight into the story that so informed my childhood years.

Jesus lived thirty-three years on this planet, but the occasions we celebrate most of all are his birth and his death. What is it that links these two momentous events?

He was born in a stable. There was no hospital with doctors and nurses in attendance; no clean bed with white sheets for his mother to lie in; no warm water or towels available to wash and dry him. His parents were not married; Joseph was not even the father; they were on the run and under threat of death from Herod's soldiers; there was no comfort and no safety. It seems to me that symbolically this is as clear a description of being born vulnerable as one can get.

The story of Jesus' birth reminds us that our birthright is vulnerability. Take a newborn baby and leave it alone and it will surely die. We are dependent on the adults around us to take care of us - much longer than for any other species. We need attention, approval and affection to survive and thrive. The theory of the Psychology of Selves tells us that our primary selves develop to protect this core vulnerability. They have us behave in ways designed to get our survival needs met in our particular family, society and culture. As these protector selves develop, so our vulnerability often gets buried and forgotten.

At his death, was Jesus in the comfort of his own bed in his own home? Were his friends and family by his bedside? Was his doctor close by to relieve his pain? No. He was betrayed, stripped naked and had a crown of thorns pushed onto his head. He was paraded through jeering crowds, hauling a heavy cross on his back. He was nailed up for all to see, with the most vulnerable parts of his body totally exposed. It was a brutal and public death and again symbolically a painfully clear description of dying vulnerable.

The story of his death reminds us that our "deathright" is vulnerability. As we age and our bodies start to deteriorate our primary protecting selves cannot handle situations as they once did - our energy and stamina decline, our memory begins to fail us, and our actions slow. This causes our vulnerability to resurface and be felt. We are the only animal on the planet that knows some day we must die. No matter what our belief system may be about death, we have no proof as to what happens to us once we depart. This not knowing can't but prick our vulnerability.

For me, Christmas and Easter are reminders that we are born and die vulnerable. It is an essential condition of being alive and human on this planet. Vulnerability that we are unaware of or that we do not feel safe sharing with others is at the root of most conflict, so how we handle our vulnerability throughout our lives is the real issue for us. Do we identify with our primary protecting selves and disown, bury or try to forget our vulnerability? Or do we use our vulnerability as a guide to becoming fuller, more conscious human beings?

APPENDIX 1:
FACILITATION

Belly Art

In the late 1970's I spent three years living in Tokyo. During the day I earned a living travelling around the city teaching English to company employees and in the evenings I studied a martial art called *Shintaido* ("New Body Way").

One day, as the doors of my commuter train opened at Ryōgoku station, the impressive figure of a sumo wrestler stepped into the carriage. His wooden "geta" (traditional Japanese shoes) clunked noisily on the floor as he occupied a seat - or rather seats! - opposite me. His hair was tied up in a "chonmage" (topknot) and he wore a blue patterned "yukata" (summer kimono) tied with an embroidered "obi" (cotton belt) around his huge midriff.

I felt intimidated by the enormity of his presence and glanced across at him nervously. He was taller than I had imagined a sumo wrestler to be. His broad feet hung over the sides of his shoes and above his thick ankles were a pair of tree-trunk legs. Atop these rested the incredible bulk of his belly and over that his massive chest and shoulders. His round face with its small mouth seemed strangely baby-like. It was difficult to gauge his age.

I could see how, when squatting down to face his opponent in a tournament, his enormous stomach would give him great stability - like a triangle resting firmly on its base. I couldn't help comparing this to archetypal Western images of the ideal masculine physique - Superman, Mr Incredible or American football players. With their exaggerated shoulders and slim waists these popular heroes appeared more like inverted triangles balancing somewhat precariously on one point!

It was not just the sheer physical mass of his body that so impressed me. There was also something about his energy that I found fascinating. He appeared not just very grounded but also centred and he had an ineffable inner calm. Even though his eyes were half-closed and he seemed to be paying me no attention at all, I felt that there was some kind of invisible communication taking place between us. It was as if I was being scanned by an energy radiating from his belly and that he was using this to take the measure of me. After a few stops he stood up impassively and exited the train, leaving an indelible mark in my mind.

Sometime later I was invited by my Shintaido teacher to accompany him to a sumo tournament. As we watched the bouts he explained the various moves each wrestler was using to try and force his adversary to touch the ground, or step outside the "dohyō" (small circular wrestling ring).

He pointed out that there were various slapping, holding, pulling and pushing techniques, but that fundamental to them all was the ability to maintain a strong and low centre of gravity, making it very difficult to be destabilised and thrown off balance. I knew from my Shintaido training that the place in the belly where this centre is located is called the "hara", which is three finger widths below and two finger widths behind the navel.

He explained that in Japan, a master of such disciplines as calligraphy, swordsmanship, tea ceremony or the fighting arts like sumo is said to be *"acting from the hara"*. Teachers of these arts often instruct their students to centre their mind in their hara in order to anchor themselves. In addition to breathing techniques and physical exercises, developing the hara also involves emotional and spiritual practice. As a consequence, the student becomes more aware of and sensitive to both internal and external energies. Consciously communicating with someone from one's hara is called "haragei" - literally "belly art".

I listened attentively, realising that his words were not so much a description of what was going on at the tournament but more an instruction to me as I continued with my study of the martial arts.

Over the years I have applied the practical experience and understanding of hara I gained in Japan to different areas of my life - including to my work as a Voice Dialogue facilitator.

Like the sumo wrestler, when I facilitate clients I have to be both centred and grounded. Focusing down into my hara helps me to "scan" my clients and be sensitive to the different selves that show up during sessions. Identifying and resonating the energy of these selves from my hara helps clients deepen their experience of a particular self. The greater my capacity to consciously hold as many selves as possible "in my belly", the better able I will be to facilitate the wonderful variety of selves my clients present.

My goal as a facilitator is, however, very different from that of the sumo wrestler. When working with clients my job is to help them become aware of, stand between and embrace as many of their selves as they can. The natural consequence of this for the client is a feeling of being more expanded, centred and grounded. Far from trying to destabilise and throw my clients off balance, my task is to help them do the opposite - to become more stable and more in balance.

I have always found the Japanese depiction of Hotei (the so-called Laughing or Fat Buddha) attractive. I love the rotund figures with their big bellies and broadly smiling faces. When I look at them I am reminded of my first encounter with that sumo wrestler on the train at Ryōgoku and of the words of my teacher: *"It is in the hara that the soul of a man resides."*

A Voice Dialogue Session

A Voice Dialogue session might take an hour or more. The form is quite simple. The client sits opposite the facilitator and moves his or her chair to different places in order to access the different selves that wish to speak. After talking to a self the client moves back to the starting place - the Aware Ego. The facilitator's skill lies in helping the client experience each self fully and then separate from it. In a typical session the facilitator may talk to three or four different selves.

It is important to understand that Voice Dialogue is not a technique for getting rid of any part of us. Rather, it is a natural and inclusive process that enables us to embrace and respect all of the many selves that exist inside us without making any of them wrong. It is safe because we always talk first to the primary self that is in charge of keeping the client secure - for example, a Protector or Controller self - and get its permission to go ahead with the session. We never try to circumvent or violate the rules of the primary selves. Each session unfolds at the client's own pace.

Having dialogued with a particular set of selves and given them voice, the client is now able to stand between them with more awareness, not flip-flopping and being pulled first in one direction and then the other.

Voice Dialogue gives us an opportunity to find a place of calm consideration and discernment rather than visceral judgement or unconscious reaction. It enables us to step back from our habitual ways of being and doing, and therefore have more choice in how we handle what life brings us.

To see two demonstrations sessions go to:

Neil: http://vimeo.com/4102934

Maryline: http://vimeo.com/4226016

APPENDIX 2:
GLOSSARY

Voice Dialogue

Voice Dialogue is a method for entering into direct communication with your inner community of selves. Each self or sub-personality is addressed with full recognition of both its individual importance and its role as only a part of the total personality.

The Psychology of Selves

This is the name that Drs Hal and Sidra Stone have given to the theoretical framework for Voice Dialogue. It describes the development of the different selves; the interaction of the selves with one another; and the relationship between the selves of two people or *bonding patterns*. It also includes the three levels of their consciousness model: *Awareness, Experience of the Selves, and the Aware Ego Process.*

Primary Self

This is a self that is dominant in the personality and one that a person is identified with. There is an initial primary self that develops in infancy or early childhood called the Protector/Controller or Security-Guard. Other typical primary selves for Westerners are: the Rule-Maker, the Critic, the Pusher, the Pleaser, and the Perfectionist. As a person matures, other selves develop or come forward, so a primary self may be current but not initial.

Protector/Controller or Security Guard

This part is the first of the primary selves to develop to protect the Vulnerable-Child and to control the child's behaviour in an effort to gain whatever attention, approval and affection is available from those around the child.

Primary Selves System

This consists of the Protector/Controller or Security-Guard and the other primary selves (the Rule-Maker, the Critic, the Pusher, etc.) that it encouraged to develop to protect the child and to support its aims and aspirations. This system sets the tone and value structure of the personality. There can be the *initial* primary selves system and the *current* primary selves system. For example: an original conservative system and a current liberal or "new-age" one.

Disowned Self

This is a self that represent the opposite value structure from a primary self. These are the selves that had to be rejected or hidden in the growing up process.

Disowned Instinctual Selves

These are selves that have been so deeply buried that they have taken on a highly charged energy. They are very threatening to the primary selves system. When they come out they can cause the primary selves lots of anxiety and problems - as when a normally mild mannered person becomes violent or verbally vicious under the influence of alcohol.

Bonding Patterns

The interaction between two people, or groups of people, that replicates the original parent-child bonding of infancy. Bonding patterns are as natural and normal as breathing. A bonding pattern can feel good - "positive" - or feel bad - "negative".

- Positive Bonding Pattern

In this form of interaction each person meets the other person's needs. The child self in each person is taken care of by a parental self in the other. These patterns are predictable and safe.

- Negative Bonding Pattern

In this type of interaction one or both partners' feelings have been hurt and the primary selves jump in to protect the underlying vulnerability. You no longer feel safe, mutual respect disappears, and judgements start to fly.

Acting or Operating Ego

This is an ego that is identified with the primary selves system. This identification can shift throughout one's lifetime. For example: at the age of twenty-five you may still be identified with the original selves that might be conservative in the sense of having attitudes like, "Keep a smile on your face", "Don't let anyone see you crying", "Act tough", "Make sure everyone likes you". After a few years in a personal growth or recovery program, your ego may become identified with a "new-age" Protector/Controller or Security Guard that values, "Letting it all hang out". Often the selves of the initial primary system then become the current disowned selves.

Aware Ego Process

Every time you access and then separate from a primary or disowned self you enter into and strengthen the Aware Ego. For example, if you are strongly identified with a Pusher self and then you separate from it, the "you" that began the Voice Dialogue session is no longer the same "you" because you are no longer identified with your Pusher. You are then free to go to the other side and access your Easy-Going self, understand its motivation and then separate from it. When you come back to centre you are again a new "you" - one that is now no longer identified with your Pusher or with your Easy-Going self. Resting between this pair of opposites is the Aware Ego.

The Aware Ego is constantly in process - a process of learning to stand in the space between opposites. Since there are literally hundreds of opposite selves, the process is a dynamic one and continually evolving.

APPENDIX 3:
FURTHER INFORMATION

Bibliography

Embracing Our Selves

Hal Stone & Sidra Stone

New World Library

Embracing Each Other

Hal Stone & Sidra Stone

New World Library

Embracing Your Inner Critic

Hal Stone & Sidra Stone

Harper San Francisco

The Shadow King: The Invisible Force That Holds Women Back

Sidra Stone

Nataraj Publishing

Partnering: A New Kind of Relationship

Hal Stone & Sidra Stone

Nataraj Publishing

The Fireside Chats

Hal Stone & Sidra Stone

Delos, inc.

The Energetics of Voice Dialogue

Robert Stamboliev

LifeRhythm

The Self Behind the Symptom

Judith Hendin

Lulu

Websites

Voice Dialogue UK:

www.voicedialogue.org.uk

The Voice Dialogue Online Program:

www.voicedialogueonline.com

Voice Dialogue International:

www.voicedialogue.org

Videos

John Interviews Voice Dialogue Practitioners:
http://www.youtube.com/user/JKVDUK/videos

John Interviewed on Conscious TV:
http://link.brightcove.com/services/player/bcpid1321306269?bctid=712
50818001

About the Author

Born in London, John has lived and worked as a communication trainer, seminar leader and facilitator in Europe, Africa, Asia, South America and USA. He has over thirty years experience in developing and delivering intensive seminars that help participants improve both intra-personal and interpersonal communication. He has worked with corporate, academic, medical and scientific organizations as well as many private clients.

John has studied Voice Dialogue with its creators, Drs. Hal & Sidra Stone in the USA and Europe. From 1991 to 1995 he co-founded the Voice Dialogue Centre of Tucson, Arizona and taught Voice Dialogue in San Francisco.

He is now based in London where he conducts Voice Dialogue workshops and private sessions with individuals and couples face to face and via skype. His latest venture is the creation of the first Voice Dialogue Online Program, enabling people worldwide to learn at distance about Voice Dialogue, The Psychology of Selves and the Aware Ego Process.

Contact him at:
www.voicedialogue.org.uk
info@voicedialogue.org.uk

4572342R00065

Printed in Great Britain
by Amazon.co.uk, Ltd.,
Marston Gate.